PRIVATE GARDEN

TENDER PROPHETIC WORDS TO ENCOURAGE YOU

DAVE WILLIAMS

PRIVATE GARDEN

Tender Prophetic Words to Encourage You

Unless otherwise noted, all Scripture quotations are taken from the King James Version of the Bible.

ISBN 0-938020-88-9

First Printed 2007

Cover designed by Timothy Henley

Published by:

DECAPOLIS
PUBLISHING

Printed in the United States of America

OTHER BOOKS BY DAVE WILLIAMS

ABC's of Success and Happiness
Angels: They Are Watching You
Beatitudes: Success 101
The Beauty of Holiness
Coming Into the Wealthy Place
The Desires of Your Heart
Developing the Spirit Of a Conqueror
Emerging Leaders
End-Times Bible Prophecy
Faith Goals
Filled
Genuine Prosperity
Gifts That Shape Your Life and Change Your World
Have You Heard From the Lord Lately
How to Be a High Performance Believer
How to Help Your Pastor Succeed
The Jezebel Spirit
Miracle Results of Fasting
The New Life . . . The Start of Something Wonderful
Pacesetting Leadership
The Presence of God
The Pastor's Minute
Radical Fasting
Radical Forgiveness
Radical Healing
The Road to Radical Riches
Regaining Your Spiritual Momentum
Seven Sign-Posts on the Road to Spiritual Maturity
Somebody Out There Needs You
What to Do if You Miss the Rapture
The World Beyond
Your Pastor: A Key To Your Personal Wealth
36 Minutes With the Pastor

TABLE OF CONTENTS

PART I

SECRETS FROM HEAVEN

SECRETS FROM HEAVEN

- Secrets from Heaven are now coming to earth.
- Strategic plans from Heaven are being transmitted and are available at this moment.
- Fresh prophetic light is speeding forth by God's Spirit to those who are ready and willing to receive.
- God is speaking, and you want to be in the right place at the right time listening to Him.

GOD HAS A VOICE

Over the past three decades, the Lord has spoken to me on many occasions, sometimes gently and at other times dramatically. It has always been my practice to record my encounters in a journal. I maintain a daily record of my Bible reading and those things the Holy Spirit chooses to reveal to me.

I have never been inclined to publish any of the prophetic words I've heard from the Lord. First, I didn't want people to equate these "words" with the Holy Scriptures. Second, I was concerned that people may tend to look to prophetic words as a source of strength more than God's written Word—the Bible. And third, I do not consider myself to be a prophet. I'm just a simple follower of Jesus Christ, God's Son.

As a young believer, I was happy to learn that God has a voice and still speaks today. If you'd like an in-depth study on this subject, get a copy of my book, ***Have You Heard from the Lord Lately?*** In discovering God's voice, I came to an awareness of how He speaks to His people through revelation and prophetic-like "words." I've heard the audible voice of God only once in thirty some years, but I've heard the voice of His Spirit, in the depths of my spirit, on many occasions.

God's written Word—the Bible—gives us God's general will for everyone. God's Spirit, who lives in every born-again believer, gives God's specific will to us. He does this by creating desires in our hearts to do certain things, or perhaps by an inner urging. As we look at the New Testament Church, we find the disciples were constantly guided by the Holy Spirit and listening for His voice.

> One day as they were worshiping God—they were also fasting as they waited for guidance—the Holy Spirit spoke: "Take Barnabas and Saul and commission them for the work I have called them to do."
>
> **—Acts 13:2 (MSG)**

> There was a disciple in Damascus by the name of Ananias. The Master spoke to him in a vision: "Ananias." "Yes, Master?" he answered. "Get up and go over to Straight Avenue. Ask at the house of Judas for a man from Tarsus. His name is Saul. He's there praying. He has just had a dream in which he saw a man named Ananias enter the house and lay hands on him so he could see again."
>
> **—Acts 9:10-12 (MSG)**

> And when he was come unto us, he took Paul's girdle, and bound his own hands and feet, and said, Thus saith the Holy Ghost, So shall the Jews at Jerusalem bind the man that owneth this girdle, and shall deliver him into the hands of the Gentiles.
>
> **—Acts 21:11**

> Now we have received, not the spirit of the world, but the spirit which is of God; that we might know the things that are

freely given to us of God. Which things also we speak, not in the words which man's wisdom teacheth, but which the Holy Ghost teacheth; comparing spiritual things with spiritual. But the natural man receiveth not the things of the Spirit of God: for they are foolishness unto him: neither can he know them, because they are spiritually discerned.

—1 Corinthians 2:12-14

EARS TO HEAR WHAT THE SPIRIT IS SAYING

Anyone with ears to hear must listen to the Spirit and understand what he is saying to the churches.

—Revelation 2:17a (NLT)

As I sit in the morning and read the Bible, God sometimes enlightens and personalizes certain passages so strongly to me, I feel compelled to write them down as the Spirit of God prompts, and they become prophetic words to me. I've done this for over thirty years now.

For example, here's a prophetic "word" straight out of my journal from my time in the "private garden" with the Lord. I thought it would be a perfect introduction to this book.

A "WORD" FROM MY JOURNAL

"Come now, My beloved child, and we shall meet in the private garden. I will whisper wonderful things to your open heart—things that you do not yet know. Yes, I will unveil My plans for you and uncover My blueprint of things yet to come in your life.

"Do not be afraid, My love. In the private garden you are safe. My perfect love will cast out all your fears. You will bask in My peace—a peace this world cannot provide to you.

"Ask me those deep, perplexing questions that have vexed your soul, causing you unrest and sometimes anger. Ask me, and out of the far stretches of eternity I will speak. Yes, I will speak as I am speaking to you now, and only those who make the time to meet Me in the private garden shall be able to hear My voice and give heed.

"You choose a good thing, my love, when you come to meet Me in the private garden. This is the place where I impart divine revelation—a heavenly knowledge and wisdom that makes the wisdom of the world seem foolish and inconsequential. Many are chasing after things that bring only emptiness and more emptiness. They never arrive at the place of real fulfillment because they never arrive at the private garden. Only those who come and wait in the garden of My presence, shall find eternal pleasure and joys evermore. Yes, My love, you have chosen a good thing.

"Come now and get cozy. Allow Me to unlock My treasury of wisdom to your heart. Let Me speak a healing word to you. Permit Me to hush the agitations in your life and speak words of peace to your soul. Let Me lock out all the thoughts that are unworthy of the private garden. Let Me unlock the mystery of My peace, joy, and nature. In the private garden, I will give you a special and valuable gift—the gift of wisdom and the gift of miracles. Yes, in this spot, I will pour out answers for those things that seem impossible.

"Talking to my friends on the road to Emmaus, did not their hearts burn within them as I spoke? Did they not go on to affect every generation? You too, My beloved child, will find your heart burning within you as you listen to My words in the private garden. And you, too, will move forward in faith and perform exploits in My name that will affect entire families, cities, and even nations.

"Those who do not value the private garden of My presence, will only possess unrealized fantasies. Here I will give you dreams and visions that will surely come to pass. I purchased this glorious gift for you with My own blood. Now take advantage of all the gifts I freely give to you. Meet Me in the private garden, My love."

Digging Out The Old Journals

In the past few years, I dug out all my old journals and re-read some of the prophetic words God revealed to my heart. They are still as fresh and relevant today as when I originally received them and wrote them in my journal. They spoke comfort and direction to me regarding situations I was facing. Some of these "words" provided solutions to struggles I was facing. As I re-read them, they refreshed me once again.

I had my secretary type out a few of these prophetic words. I had never shared these words with anyone—not even my wife. However, I wanted to encourage a group of ministers I was meeting with, so I gave them about twelve of the prophetic words I had received from God over the years. Their response was extraordinary. Each "word" was perfect for a situation each leader was facing. They encouraged me to publish them.

I was reluctant for the reasons I already mentioned. Yet now, four years after these leaders encouraged me to print the prophetic words, I find myself doing it with the simple goal of encouraging, comforting, and lifting you *in a time of special need.*

You'll find these prophetic words inspiring and anointed, but you must remember they are ***not*** equivalent with Scriptures.

My Strategic Global Mission partners receive one prophetic word every month with their receipt, and they have been blessed. I can't count the number of times a partner has said to me, "It was just what I needed," or "It was a blessing and an answer to prayer."

What Is A Prophetic Word?

When you face a difficult situation that has no textbook solution, you need a prophetic word. Just one prophetic word from the Lord can bring faith, power, resolve, confirmation, repentance, or simple answers to your desperate questions.

My friend John was facing a critical situation where he stood to lose several thousand dollars in an out-of-state land deal. The situation looked hopeless. There was absolutely no answer. That's when John visited the "private garden" as he walked alone down the street, seeking God for an answer. Like a miracle, the answer came via a prophetic word—a heaven sent idea. He took action on the word, and it brought a wonderful victory to his challenge. One word from God can change everything.

Receiving a prophetic word from God is not fortune telling. It's simply going to the private garden and meeting with God so you can enjoy each other and chat with one another. When you are in your private garden—your place of communion with the Creator—He will share something with you. When you speak it forth in faith—not by your own thoughts, desires, or opinions—it becomes a prophetic word.

A prophetic word can bring you to repentance.

A prophetic word can open the door to the realm of miracles.

A prophetic word can give you guidance during a struggle, or confirmation to do, or not to do, something on your heart.

A prophetic word can bring you strength and comfort in times of confusion.

A prophetic word is a "now" word, a "today" word. My prayer is that as you read the prophetic words God has spoken to me over the years, they will be relevant "now" words for you and will bless you.

God wants to speak to each of us. Paul said, "Ye may all prophesy . . . ."

> **For ye may all prophesy one by one, that all may learn, and all may be comforted.**
>
> **—1 Corinthians 14:31**

Prayer was never meant to be merely words *to* God, but an interactive event, with words *from* God. We speak and listen. God listens and speaks.

> **. . . Call to me and I will answer you. I'll tell you marvelous and wondrous things that you could never figure out on your own.**
>
> **—Jeremiah 33:3b (MSG)**

God speaks to me mostly through His Word, which I love. Yet at times, He speaks to me strongly by His Spirit, and when He does, it always harmonizes with—and never contradicts—the written Word of God.

My place of daily prayer is like a private garden for me. When Adam and Eve lived in the Garden of Eden, they had daily walks and talks with God. Their sin disrupted that fellowship. Thankfully Jesus, through His death and resurrection, brought us back to the Garden, so to speak.

WHY THIS BOOK IS NAMED "PRIVATE GARDEN"

God must love gardens. After all, He created man and placed him in a lush, peaceful garden—The Garden of Eden. Jesus often spoke in agricultural terms. "The sower went out to sow his seed . . . ." ". . . If you have faith as a grain of mustard seed . . . ." He even speaks of His Father as being a Gardener in John 15.

> **I am the true vine, and My Father is the vinedresser.**
>
> **— John 15:1 (NKJV)**

There's something special about a serene garden, beautifully landscaped, filled with luxurious flowers, trees, and plants.

Couples love to have their wedding ceremonies in special gardens. In the Song of Solomon, the special lover is called a "secret garden."

> **Dear lover and friend, you're a secret garden, a private and pure fountain.**
>
> **—Song of Solomon 4:8 (MSG)**

We live in a fast-paced society. We get more data and information in a day than our ancestors digested in their entire lifetime. We face daily agitations, disruptions, and provocations.

God placed man in a garden, not a twisted, gnarly jungle. Jesus loved to retreat to His private resort in the garden, just outside of the city, where He would meet with His Father.

We Yearn For A Private Place

Sometimes we long for a place—any place—with the solitude of a private garden with a bubbling brook. We long to just get away from the hustle and bustle of life. When we have questions, we would like to meet a friend with all the answers.

There is such a place, and there is such a Friend. He has the answers to all of life's questions, and He waits for you daily in the private garden. He offers you a place where you are free from the storms of life, a resort with extraordinary peace—a quiescent, tranquil garden where God wraps His arms around you and speaks words of comfort and encouragement to your thirsty heart.

The private garden is an intimate, cozy place.

The private garden is a meeting spot where you get inside information, which is called "revelation." And when you *speak* the revelation, it becomes a prophetic word.

Would you like to know what the future holds for you?

> **Howbeit when he, the Spirit of truth, is come, he will guide you into all truth: for he shall not speak of himself; but whatsoever he shall hear, that shall he speak: and he will shew you things to come.**
>
> **—John 16:13**

Someone waits daily for you to arrive at the private garden to talk about important things that will affect your future. God, Himself, is waiting to show you great and mighty things.

> **But as it is written, Eye hath not seen, nor ear heard, neither have entered into the heart of man, the things which God hath prepared for them that love him. But God hath revealed them**

> **unto us by his Spirit: for the Spirit searcheth all things, yea, the deep things of God.**
>
> **—1 Corinthians 2:9-10**

MAY I SUGGEST?

My prayer is that each of these prophetic words will speak to you in a significant and helpful way. And further, my prayer is that you will daily retreat to the private garden to chat with God and learn to receive revelation from Him to speak prophetically and powerfully.

I'd like to suggest the following:

1. ***Stay humble.*** God speaks to the humble but withholds from the arrogant and proud. Don't go around telling everyone, "God told me this," and "God told me that." Ask the Lord for special grace and humility when He gives you a prophetic word.

2. ***Keep a journal.*** It can be a one-dollar spiral notebook or an expensive leather bound luxury journal.

3. ***Go to your private garden daily.***

4. ***Read God's Word daily.*** The Bible will keep you on the right path and protect you from any false words the devil may try to implant. Ask the Holy Spirit to personalize it for you, and reveal any principle or truth He wants you to know.

5. ***Ask God questions.*** Ask Him for wisdom and solutions, and He will give them to you.

6. ***Keep a record*** of the ideas, thoughts, and words the Lord may give to you during these times.

Remember, enjoy your own private garden every day. God is waiting for you. He can hardly wait to show you great and mighty things that you don't yet know.

Please be encouraged and challenged by some of the prophetic words the Lord has spoken to my heart during times of fellowship in my personal "Private Garden."

"God, Himself, is waiting to show you great and mighty things."

"The Bible will keep you on the right path and protect you from any false words the devil may try to implant."

PART II

PROPHETIC WORDS FROM THE PRIVATE GARDEN

1

FOUR IMPORTANT INSTRUCTIONS

Today, My precious one, I need to speak to you concerning some important matters that will have significant impact upon your life, your relationships, and your work. Harken to My Spirit, and you shall gain poise and strength, even in the midst of what appears to be unfavorable and treacherous circumstances.

First, know this: I am your refuge and strength, and I have placed you under My everlasting arms.

Second, remember that I have purposed for you to live your life one day at a time. No two days are ever exactly the same. Worry not about your yesterdays. I know all about them, and My grace is sufficient to take care of them. Fret not about tomorrow. My grace will take care of all your tomorrows. Tomorrow is in My hands; I have not given it to you yet. At this moment, I am tailoring your tomorrows for your good, so you need not succumb to foreboding and anxiety. You cannot live your whole life today, so enjoy My daily bread today, for I have given you strength for today.

Third, I have fashioned into every soul the need for a refuge, a place to go when facing trouble and pressure. You, beloved, must have a temporal refuge of solitude and quietness—a place to restore your soul. Your enemy is a relentless hound, and you need to come away to the secret place where I, the Lord, will show Myself strong on your behalf as your eternal refuge.

Fourth, trust Me when you are facing scary and terrifying experiences. These things, though uncomfortable, are preparing you to soar as an eagle with vision, strength, and speed. I am preparing you to navigate through the currents of life. I won't let you fall. I haven't forgotten where you are. You are under My everlasting arms.

My precious child, with the eternal God as your refuge and strength, you shall tread on serpents and scorpions and not be harmed. You will be able to take on anything and emerge with the heavenly scent of victory.

Remember these words and tuck them into your heart, and you shall rise above every difficulty, challenge, and obstacle with a peace and poise others won't understand. You are My child, and you are under My protective arms. Always remember that, beloved.

". . . I am your refuge and strength, and I have placed you under My everlasting arms."

2

CARES

My darling child, listen to My gentle voice and do not neglect My teachings. Cherish our times together as you read My Word and listen to My Spirit.

You are often troubled by the cares of this life that make Me *seem* distant rather than close to you. Remember child, the cares of this life have the power to choke My Word, making it ineffectual in its power to bless, profit, and bring about a miracle change.

Yes, your enemy has spread a net for you—a trap, a snare. He brings to your mind worries, fears, and anxieties that I never intended for you. Step around those wicked snares, and let My Words penetrate your heart with a joyful power.

Do not ignore My advice and warnings. I generously pour out My Spirit in you to make known My ways which lead to life, power, wisdom, and favor. Follow My Words, not your own schemes, or the pressures from others who compromise My will. Allow My Spirit to speak to you through My Word, which I have exalted even above My Name.

If you harken to My tender voice of love toward you, dread, disaster, and calamity will remain far from you, and treasures beyond your finite grasp will break forth upon you. My darling child, treasure our times together, and receive My wisdom for your complete victory.

3

MORE THAN YOU CAN ASK

My child, you know I am able to accomplish infinitely more than you ask or imagine. You know I have placed My mighty power in you to work great and glorious things. Why then do you fret over the insults and threats of your enemies?

Yes, I will scatter those who have set themselves against you, and whose words are always stirring up trouble for you. I will put them on the run, humiliate them, lower them to the ground, and haul them away in shame and dishonor. Calamity and disaster will overtake them in a moment; while honor, mercy and favor will overtake you . . . as you put your trust in My Word.

You have spoken the truth and declared only what is right. Know this My child; I cared for you before you were born while you were still in your mother's womb. I have watched over you and carried you along to this point. Do you think I will desert you now?

While your enemies stagger under the weight of their deceptions, unprepared for what will suddenly take them by surprise, I will protect you and guard My mighty name. They will be stricken without pity, but you, My dear one, will hear My gentle voice and continue your special work with humility and gentleness. I will whisper mysteries to your heart that are entirely new to you and show you many great things—things you do not yet know.

I will teach you and guide you. I have not forgotten you—not at all. I will not forget you, even when you feel deserted. I am teaching you to trust not in what you see, hear, and feel but to trust in My everlasting Word.

All who are trying to destroy you will go away in shame. Yes, they will trickle away; their nakedness, deceptions, and shame will be exposed. They are not prepared for what I am planning. Yet even now, if they would turn to Me, I would forgive them, heal them, and give them a place of honor. Soon, the strike will be made; it will be too late for them. They will get no help from their friends—no help at all. All their friends, who also walk in deception, will go their own ways, turning a deaf ear to their cries.

They love their guilty ways; because of it, they shall be crushed beneath the mighty power of My Truth. Yet you, My beloved, will have peace flowing like a gentle river. I will make you a light to those who have no light, a deliverer to those who are imprisoned.

When you trust Me, and the power of My Word, you will never be put to shame. I am giving you words of wisdom and opening your understanding to My plans. Who dares to bring a charge against My anointed? Who dares accuse My beloved? You will look and say, "Where are my accusers?" Then you will be shaken when you see their lives eaten away like old clothes that have been eaten by moths.

So do not fret My beloved. My power is working in you, and you will see all I have announced come to pass. You will grow stronger and stronger each day as you follow the example of your Lord Jesus.

4

A CHOSEN LEADER

My dear child, yes, I have chosen you for a high position of leadership in My family. You have been placed strategically to motivate My people and energize them in My purposes with honesty and a strong moral foundation.

There are those who have called themselves "leaders," yet have wreaked havoc in countless lives with their smooth, charming but dishonest speeches. Stay clear of these types, My child, for I have appointed you to wisdom, truth, and trust.

You shall lead many thirsty souls to springs of fresh water as you trust Me and develop an eagerness to drink in more of My truth daily. Your words are anointed to heal and help, even when, at times, they seem strong. Do not fear man. Do not be afraid to speak the words I whisper to your heart.

You shall be My reliable reporter, announcing what My Spirit says to the Church. Your words will be like a fountain of life and a healing presence as you trust Me and speak what My Spirit says to your spirit.

These others, who love their titles more than their time with Me, speak careless words from their own imaginations, and wonder why they evoke nothing from their hearers. They are pretentious, showy, and empty.

But your words, as you speak them in faith, are simple and full of life because they come from My Word, My heart, My

Spirit. I can't stomach liars. And week after week, day after day, I hear pretenders saying, "God told me; God showed me; God spoke," when I haven't so much as whispered in their direction.

You My child, will never lay down the smoke screen of deceit, for My truth is the only truth that lasts eternally. Jesus said, "Heaven and earth shall pass away, but My words last forever." Therefore, in faith speak My words, and you shall bless your city as well as many nations. In return, I will bless you with honor and wealth. You motivate and invigorate My people to flee apathy and lethargy, and to follow My principles in all honesty and sincerity, and I will reward you immensely.

"Do not fear man. Do not be afraid to speak the words I whisper to your heart."

5

LISTEN

Pay close attention to Me, dear one. Take My Words, and plant them in your heart. Seek My wisdom as if it were a hidden treasure, and you will be guarded and protected by it.

So many times you have felt that darkness was over your life, and Heaven was silent. My precious one, I am here now to speak words of great victory—words to lead you in the pathway of what is right according to My perfect plan.

You are My child, and My plan and desire is to grant you a long life with good years and peace from the turmoil and anguish you have known. Remember My mercy every day for it is fresh and new for you each morning. Do not depend on human understanding, for it is faulty and will fail you in time.

I admonish those I love. Therefore, I admonish you, dear one, to pay close attention to Me. Seek My wisdom; hear My words; forget not My merciful benefits. Then you will be guarded day and night from all the wicked schemes of your enemy. Yes, and you will find peace and success in your journey.

Look for Me today. Listen for My voice. Watch for My priceless wisdom and guidance. When you do these things, you will enjoy all My benefits, and the turmoil and anguish you have known will be in the past.

6

DISTRACTIONS

Be still, and know that I am God. There remains a rest for My people. Discover My rest and enter into it.

My child, there are so many people, things, and events screaming for your attention, but I have ordained only a few of them. They call for and demand your time, robbing you of the peace and rest that I have mandated for you.

You are not the Holy Spirit. You cannot be in more than one place, doing more than one thing at the same time. Yet you try. You feel such pressure from all sides to do this, do that, go here, go there. You moan, "Oh where has the sense of God's presence gone? Where is my joy? Why am I so fatigued and exhausted?"

The answer lies with you. You accept too many "things." You have agreed to do things and attend events I have not called you to. You are drained and weary. A dullness of spirit, like a parasite, bores its way into your being.

Distractions are everywhere; they trap you and cause you to grow faint. You are running, but never getting any closer to the finish line because you've been distracted—stopping here and pausing there. There are so many voices on the sidelines in your race, but only My voice will instruct you toward rest and victory.

Humble yourself and rest by sitting before Me; allow Me to lift you, re-energize you, and restore the peace you once enjoyed. Stop activities that pull you from the race I have set before you. Wait on Me in tender moments of worship, for I love you and have ordained you to enjoy My peace that passes all understanding.

My yoke is easy, and My burden is light. Take upon you no other yoke—no other burden. Yes, be still and know that I am your God; in My presence is rest, peace, and fullness of joy.

"My yoke is easy, and My burden is light. Take upon you no other yoke . . . ."

7

REJOICE, REJOICE, REJOICE!

Rejoice, rejoice, rejoice, for the victory is Mine! Oh My child, you will see My salvation and deliverance, and you will not have to lift a finger against your foes. I will do it. Yes, I will do it, and you will be filled with thanksgiving and joy.

I have declared Christ and the Church are one. And those who stand against My Church are standing against My Son. Not even the strongest militia of hell can stand against My Son and My Church. Yet greedy people filled with evil intentions continue in their darkness, accusing and threatening My people. But no more, no more, no more!

Their evil intentions will be exposed. They will be utterly disgraced, humiliated, and will not inherit My kingdom.

But you, My child, rejoice, rejoice, rejoice! For your victory is secure and assured. I have spoken it and will not go back on my Word.

I will go ahead of you and protect you. I will be your rear guard, when your enemies think they are taking you by surprise. You shall prosper and be exalted because you humbled yourself before Me and trusted not in the arm of the flesh but in My Spirit and My Word.

I will flex My mighty right arm on your behalf, so rejoice, rejoice, rejoice! Shout praises to My Name. Do not fear people's scorn and rejection.

My Spirit has filled you already; act on that joy in faith by rejoicing now because I love you. Yes, like I said to Moses, My servant of old, "Stand still and see the salvation of the Lord."

Oh My child, rejoice. Let rejoicing shine on your face, in your smile, and in your actions. Speak of My glory and power. Possess My promises in their fullness. The deep waters will not swallow you, for I am already there!

So, rejoice, rejoice, rejoice, My dear one.

All of My armies are rejoicing with you.

"For your victory is secure and assured . . . . I will go ahead of you and protect you."

8

TRAPS

My beloved, beware of your enemy's snares. He has carefully set them along your path and disguised them in order to deceive you.

Often you have prayed, "Deliver me from temptation," and truly, I do make a way of escape from every temptation and trouble you face. Nonetheless, I must caution you, My child, that the traps you are looking for are often not the traps your enemy has laid out for you. Remember, he is subtle and endeavors to pull you from your simple love and pure devotion toward Jesus Christ.

Listen. Harken to Me now. I will show you the subtle snares that you must avoid. You are in a race—a marathon—and I have ordained that you will win. Becoming ensnared may not be spiritually fatal, but it will be an impediment to your race and will injure your success.

Turn your ear and your heart to My Words. Shun subtle entanglements, secret snares, and harmful traps, and you will run your race victoriously.

Major casualties do not begin as outward expressions of disobedience. No, no, no! There is first a seed that grows until it takes root and gets out of control. Here are those subtle seeds that must be uprooted daily to avoid a humiliating casualty:

Pride	Arrogance
Conceit	Greed
Covetousness	Dishonesty
Deceptive words	Stubbornness
Disharmony	Twisted attitude

The devil has many "respectable" sounding names for these casualty seeds. I will reveal them as you seek Me daily. Your enemy renames these land mines so they sound good and healthy. For example, many have stumbled and fallen out of their race because of pride, arrogance and conceit. The foe has camouflaged these casualty seeds under the guise of "self esteem," "self-confidence," and "self-image." Beware, shun, and avoid these seeds, these traps, and these life-destroying snares. Remember, without Me you can do nothing. I am here to give you the strength and power to run your race faster than you ever could alone. I have anointed you and called you to total victory.

Only by My Spirit shall you have the necessary discernment to recognize the snares set along your path.

I am here for you everyday to direct you around these traps. Look to Me, trust Me, call upon Me with a pure and open heart. I will guide you around the destructive snares, and you shall run the race and finish well.

9

ANSWERED PRAYER

My child, I will answer your prayer because you trust in Me.

I have ordained you to open the eyes of those who are blinded to My Truth, to turn them from darkness to light, from the power of Satan to the power of My Son Jesus. Trust me to use you as My instrument in these perilous days.

I offer forgiveness to all who are willing to receive, and I will give them a special place among My people, just as I have done for you. But you, My child, must call them to turn away from their sins and wicked ways, and point them to My love as expressed at Calvary in My Son. You will see changes in them, but you must be patient with them as parents are patient with their child learning to walk.

Do not fear that some will listen to others more than they listen to you. It happened to my servant Paul on more than one occasion. Do you remember the ship that set sail against Paul's warning? The ship was lost, but all life was spared. It will be the same for those who do not listen to My Words through you. They will lose much, but will be spared to listen again.

Find your special place in My body, the Church. Be connected. Be reliable. Become trusted, and I will launch you into a fresh realm of My answers. You will become more and more powerful because My armies will back you up, and I will give you great victories. You must not run and hide, but speak My Word daily.

Yes, I will answer your prayers and will grant peace and success to all who help you.

My chosen one, tell of My wondrous works, proclaim the marvelous things I have done, be filled with joy and sing praises to My Name, for I am answering you.

"I offer forgiveness to all . . . and I will give them a special place among My people . . . ."

10

A PRIZED SPOKESPERSON

You are My cherished and prized spokesperson. I have called you to speak forth My word faithfully. Do not envy those who foolishly promote their own prophetic dreams. What is the chaff to the wheat?

I have ordained you to be an overseer of multitudes, to teach them My ways, to show them My plans and purposes. I have appointed you to bring living truth to the hearts of My followers, to give them knowledge and understanding, and to lead them into My presence where everything they need is found along with immeasurable joy.

I, the Lord God, will give you the right words at the right time to break down rigid defenses and bring a sweet refreshing to the souls of your listeners. Therefore, speak; I say, speak! Open your mouth wide. I will fill it with words so powerful they will disable all human opinions and the arrogant plans of those who are walking in rebellion.

When you speak, you'll have something worthwhile to say, and you will always say it in a kind manner as you listen to My Spirit. I will give you class, My precious spokesperson, real class. I'll pour into you a new elegance and fresh dignity as you speak for Me.

Many walk in futile illusions. You My child, I have hand picked to walk in My vision. While others dream fantasies, you will stay motivated in My Word, and I will put a fire in your soul that cannot be quenched.

As you nourish yourself in My Word, trust My Son Jesus, and harken to the voice of My Spirit, I will build you up, and you shall overflow with My anointing. You will enjoy the harvest and the fruit My Word has wrought. You will sing My praises, and the angels will cheer you on. Your face will beam with My glory, and I will keep a careful eye on you, never allowing you to slip or become disobedient. I will give you more than enough of everything you need to accomplish what I've called you to do.

What is the chaff to the wheat? My Word is the wheat—nourishing, feeding, and satisfying the hunger in people's souls. Stick with My Word, and My Word will stick with you.

You are My cherished and prized spokesperson.

"I will give you more than enough of everything you need to accomplish what I've called you to do."

11

WORDS

My precious one, I want to speak to you concerning your words. As you have heard before, the power of death and life is in the tongue.

Many times you have relayed "news" from sources that have no insight into the secret world of My Spirit. You have spoken words that were contrary to My Word, often without realizing it. You have at times repeated "reports" that were out of harmony with the report of the Lord.

My child, I have ordained for you numerous blessings that have been unable to penetrate the invisible, secret wall your words have constructed around you. But today, that wall will begin to disintegrate as you speak words of faith in harmony with My authoritative and powerful Word. By My Spirit, I am prompting you each day, reminding you, encouraging you, and nudging you to possess the lips of wisdom, wherein lies the tree of life.

Yes, I have given you wise lips and a soothing tongue. I have prompted you with a gentle answer that will quiet the deepest rage in people's souls. I have called forth great treasure to fill your life as your words synchronize and harmonize with Mine.

Quiet the harsh words, the foolish words, and the deceitful words. Remember the invisible world and the invisible wall your words create. Begin now to tear down that wall which blocks My full blessings, and speak what I speak.

You have the righteousness of My Son, even when your feelings tell you otherwise. Speak My Word not your feelings. Speak your feelings only as they align with My Word.

Already, as I bear witness in your spirit, that invisible fortress around you that has stopped you from receiving my answers—created by your wrong words—is coming down by your words of faith. Spiritual brick by spiritual brick, it is crumbling to dust by the power of the fruitful words that you now speak!

Watch Me, My beloved one. Watch! You will see an increasing measure of My fullness and My favor as that invisible wall is broken. Your words, My child, have the power of curses or blessings, death or life. Speak like Me.

"Begin now to tear down that wall which blocks My full blessings, and speak what I speak."

12

A BETRAYER

My child, My precious child listen to the Lord your God. I have not stood aloof to the slander you have faced and the lies that have been spoken against you. Even some who call themselves intercessors have claimed to have "words" from My lips, but they have not. They are not intercessors but gossipers and shall receive the judgment of a slander-monger instead of the blessing of an intercessor.

There is one in particular who has fought against you. Envy and jealousy have been his motivators; they are the stingers used by the devil to gain a foothold in this person's life. While you loved, this person has fought against you and even secretly tried to destroy you. Even at the very moment when you were praying for this person, envy was eating at his soul.

He has returned evil for the good you have done for him; he has returned hatred for your love. Do not seek vengeance of any kind, for you know that vengeance is mine. At this moment, several things are happening in the spirit world. A person will turn on him and accuse him. His prayers are now being counted as sin. His years shall be few, and his position given to another who will honor Me and bless you.

Yes, his name shall become synonymous with Judas Iscariot. He refused your mercy and kindness and manipulated others with deceptions. He hounded the innocent. Instead of bringing the blessings I commanded him to bring, he brought curses. But his own curses toward you will cling to him like clothing and will be tied around him like a belt that cannot be loosed.

All who encourage him shall be disgraced; but you, My precious, *precious* child shall be encouraged and blessed. He, and all those who follow in his deception, shall be humiliated; you, My child, shall be lifted up as My humble servant. Do not seek vengeance or retaliation. Pray that he may grow a repentant heart; pray that he may be rescued from his pride and envy and the judgments to come. Do not accuse, only intercede, and I will lift you up for I am the one who gives advancement and promotion.

"Do not seek vengeance of any kind, for you know that vengeance is mine."

13

A NEW DAY

I say you have entered a NEW DAY, yes a NEW DAY.

With it, I bring you a NEW SONG.

I have brought you to this point safely, and will continue to lead you, protect you, and place a wall of My presence around you. Because of your faith and trust in the Blood of My Son, I have advanced you into a new phase—a NEW DAY.

You have entered into a NEW phase . . .

. . . a NEW phase of worshiping My Son Jesus

. . . a NEW phase of worshiping the Father

. . . a NEW phase of exuberance, delight, and joy

. . . a NEW phase of gladness

. . . a NEW phase of singing a new song

. . . a NEW phase of My presence

. . . a NEW phase of Blessings

. . . a NEW phase of gathering in the heathen

. . . a NEW phase of demonstrating My glory

. . . a NEW phase of honor

. . . a NEW phase of strength

. . . a NEW phase of beauty

. . . a NEW phase of sowing and reaping

. . . a NEW phase of generosity

. . . a NEW phase of holiness

. . . a NEW phase of fruit-bearing

. . . a NEW phase of My prosperity

. . . a NEW phase of truth and revelation

. . . a NEW phase of judgment

. . . a NEW phase of prophetic fulfillment

Yes, this is the final hour, and I shall see to it that you are a glorious Church without a spot of this world's attitudes and without a wrinkle of twisted falsehoods.

A NEW DAY! Yes, I say you have entered a NEW DAY, and I say unto you it is good.

14

THE GOOD FIGHT

My darling child, harken to My words today, and you shall experience a fresh dimension of My love, mercy, and power.

I have promised you a long, satisfying life. Yet there is an adversary roaming the earth who seeks to steal, kill, and destroy. He plots to devour the unsuspecting and unarmored soul; therefore, be vigilant and dressed for battle in My full armor.

You wrestle not against flesh and blood but against forces of the devouring adversary. This I say to you My beloved, fight the good fight of faith, and cast all your cares upon Me. Call unto Me, and I will show you My battle plans against that wicked one. Do not walk in the counsel of the ungodly, for trusting in the arm of flesh will fail. But I will not fail. I will turn your mourning into dancing.

Meditate upon My Word, for My Word is sharper than a two-edged sword that can perform divine surgery, cutting away all that is of the adversary.

I am your refuge and your help. Man's help is useless, My child. Do not fear for a moment, but look to Me and to My Words. Cry out to Me, for I have sent My Word and healed you and will send you a sign of My favor.

Resist steadfastly every instrument of the adversary. Cry out to Me. Put your confidence in Me—not man. Set a guard over the words of your mouth, for in them is the power of death and life. Speak only the things I have spoken, and your faith weapons will expand and become more powerful. Do not let your adversary steal your joy, for the joy I have placed in you shall be your strength.

Fight the good fight of faith, and you will finish your course as the adversary flees from you in terror. Jesus Christ has purchased your total victory, so be of good cheer, My precious child. You shall overcome by the Blood of the Lamb and the word of your testimony. Expect complete deliverance as you harken unto My Words.

"Speak only the things I have spoken, and your faith weapons will expand and become more powerful."

15

AN ATTACK

My child, I know when you are distressed, and I already have a solution and plan in place for you. Give thanks, for I am good and always have your best interests at heart. My love for you endures forever, and My faithfulness never ends.

You need not fear or fret. I am for you; therefore, what can mere mortals do to you? I am answering your prayers, though you hear only silence. Remember My servant Elijah? He found Me not in loud, demonstrative events, but in a still, small voice. Yes My child, I am speaking and answering your prayer; I will deliver you and set you in a large place.

There are enemies released against you, but remember you are not wrestling with flesh and blood but with spiritual creatures of wickedness. Therefore, do not trust in the arm of flesh in your time of distress, for it will fail you. It is better to put your trust in Me than to put confidence in men—even in man's armies.

Some have been hostile toward you and even attacked you in a stealth-like way. My child, I will not allow this to continue. Those who have sided with the enemy shall suffer immeasurably. I am your help and strength, but you must not lean on the arm of flesh. My strong right arm will do glorious things on your behalf, if you will but trust Me in your distress.

Yes, My child, you will sing songs of joy and victory, for I will raise you up in triumph. You will not be handed over to your enemies; you will not cave in to the pressures and distresses of the enemy. You must, My child, rest in Me by trusting Me to be your victory.

Now, My dear one, give thanks. Give thanks! Rejoice! Lift up your head, for I have purchased your redemption and your victory. Shout praise unto the Lord your God with a loud voice. Speak My Word boldly and swerve not from it. I have spoken, and I will surely do it.

"I am answering your prayers, though you hear only silence."

16

THE ASSIGNMENT

I have given you a special assignment, My dear child. Even as I assigned Paul to preach to the Gentiles and Peter to preach to the Jews, I have commissioned you for a special assignment in My Kingdom.

Many are called, but few are chosen. Yes, I have called many to a unique mission, but few will be fruitful. You ask, why? Let Me tell you, and listen with all your heart.

Many fail in their assignment because they are not faithful in the small things. They despise the seemingly insignificant daily assignments I have given them. They are not convinced that only I am the One who promotes and advances to greatness those who are reliable, available, and steadfast in the smaller assignments.

Some have natural abilities that they assume will bring them success. But My wisdom is foolishness to the natural mind. Think about this—Paul was trained and skilled in Judaism, yet I assigned him to the Gentiles. Peter was more like a Gentile than a Jew, yet I assigned him to reach the tribes of Israel. My ways are not your ways.

Others desire prominence—to be in the center, the focus of attention. They promote themselves rather than waiting for the promotion that comes not from man, but from My hand.

So, My child, here are three causes of failure in fulfilling the assignment I have given: (1) unreliability and unfaithfulness in the small things; (2) dependence on the arm of flesh, natural talents, and abilities; (3) pride, which manifests in exaltation of the self.

Your assignment, My child, will come into clarity and greater focus as you develop joy and tenacity in achieving the small things I've invited you to do. Then, as you trust Me for gifts, anointing, and the holy energizing of your natural abilities—making them supernatural—you'll see how I will move you into greater things. Finally, as you daily humble yourself before both Me and others, you'll find a divine lifting and advancement from heaven.

Yes, I have given you a special assignment that will bring great glory to the preeminent one—My Son Jesus. I have called you to a great and mighty assignment and have chosen you to succeed and be fruitful in it. Remember My words and do them; success will spring forth like the morning sun.

". . . I have called many to a unique mission, but few will be fruitful."

17

CHASING EMPTY THINGS

My beloved, do not love what is empty. Do not chase after lies as so many others do. They call good evil and evil good. They insult My honor with their longing for iniquity, tickling doctrines, and vexing lies.

They, like fools, live as if there is no God to whom they must give account. Professing themselves to be wise, and basking in their titles and airs of importance, they make themselves fools in the sight of My holy angels and My people who are called by My Name.

Do not be troubled, dear one, by their persistent resistance to My Spirit and My Word. The day is quickly approaching when they will tremble in the light of My judging presence.

You, My precious child, I have singled out to walk in My favor. I have guarded you because I know your heart is toward Me, even though you have stumbled here and there. I have ordained joy to flood your heart, light to shine in your soul, and mercy to envelop your entire being.

I take no pleasure in wickedness nor in those who perpetuate it through lies. Their throats are like open graves; but you, My dear one, have your refuge in My Son Jesus. Those arrogant "important" ones who constantly rebel against the Most High, and who persecute My people, shall not triumph in the end.

I have put My large shield around you and crowned you with My favor. The wicked will fall hard, but you will rejoice and sing with joy forever, for you have taken refuge in Jesus. Therefore, My precious child, do not follow the empty pursuits of those who are marked for swift judgment, for I have chosen you, called you, and imparted unto you true wisdom which will never fade.

"I have ordained joy to flood your heart, light to shine in your soul, and mercy to envelop your entire being."

18

CONQUEROR

Listen, My love. Listen! Open the ears of your spirit and hear the voice of My Spirit. The word of My Spirit is blowing through My Church, and a banquet is being spread to honor all My children who have become conquerors.

Don't you see? Can't you hear? When the pressures come from all sides, you are being purified and made ready for a deeper anointing and a greater advancement. But you, My love, have the power to either quit or conquer. I have ordained you to conquer, not to give up like so many others have done amidst the turmoil and pressure.

I have imparted staying power unto you—employ it diligently. Stand up, you who slouch! There is no time to waste. Stay on guard, for some who pretend to be My servants are members of the enemy's crowd and create pressure and pain for My people—My true servants. If this were not true, I would not have warned you to listen and stay on guard.

You need fear nothing, My love. You are safe from their tactics, their smear campaigns, their cold insults, and subtle lies. These enemy agents will discover the high cost of hindering My chosen ones and creating difficulty for My servants. What they mean for evil, I will turn to your good. You can be assured of that.

Listen to My Spirit. Scrape off all crustiness of heart and soul. Rest yourself in My love. Know that I am using these pressures to purify your character and to develop your patience. Don't even think about running from this test. I am spreading a wonderful banquet for those who conquer; there is a place with your name card already printed and sitting by your plate.

My Son, Jesus, never ran from the pressures brought by His enemies; He listened to My Spirit for the right words and right actions. So listen, My love. Stay alert! Be strong and courageous in My anointing. Prepare to watch Me work out every situation and to honor you as a conqueror.

"I am spreading a wonderful banquet for those who conquer . . . ."

19

DECISIONS

My beloved, I want to speak to you today. Open the ears of your heart and soul and listen attentively as I speak.

Decisions, My child, decisions! You dread acting on certain decisions because you fear making the wrong choice or offending another person. You hesitate because you fear the responsibility for the outcome. Indecision brings misery to your soul and paralyzes your thoughts.

Child, I have given you wisdom in My Son Jesus. I have blessed you with abilities and gifts. I have provided you with the freedom to make choices. Without making firm decisions, you will drift aimlessly through the precious life I have given you.

You are not a computer or a robot. You are My child, in whom I have chosen to express My love and blessings. You can make decisions founded in My wisdom and guidance. Do not retreat; do not pull back, but go forward.

Do not, My beloved, allow frustrations, nervousness, or outright fear to prevent you from following the peace I have placed in your heart. I have not given you a spirit of fear but of power, love, and a clear, sober, stable mind. Do not say, "If I'm lucky . . ." Do not surrender to superstition by flipping a coin—or some other practice engaged in by those who don't know Me.

Procrastination has consequences.

I love you and won't let you crash. Listen to My peace in your heart and follow it. Focus on Me, My darling child, by asking these questions: (1) "Am I willing to do what my Father wants no matter what?" (2) "Am I fitting into and following My Father's plans for my life?"

Act now—today—on what you already know to be My will and what I've already revealed to you by My Spirit. Your steps are ordered by Me. Before you get to step four, or step three, or step two, you must commit to taking step one. When you pursue the first step, I will begin to unveil the next step and then bring clarity to the next step after that.

Read My treasured Word, and it will profit you. Treasure My Word, and I will guide you, encourage you, and build you through My Spirit. I will show you the next step. Call unto Me, My beloved, and I will indeed show you great things you know nothing about. I will unfold your bright future. In faith, take a step. Trust me to speak to you if you are about to make a bad move or take a wrong turn. Fear not, for I will not let you fall.

Decisions have consequences. Noah made the decision to obey Me. Even though he was ridiculed, he obeyed. As a result, he and his family were spared while others suffered severe, tormenting judgment. Judas made a secret decision to betray Jesus, therefore he could not be spared the eternal torments of death and separation. Enoch made the decision to walk with Me step-by-step; because of His faith, I blessed him beyond all his contemporaries. I even took him up to heaven without him having to die.

Every decision I prompt in your life will always lead you into a deeper, fuller fellowship with My Spirit and will bring advancement and multiplication to your life, My beloved.

Decisions! Yes, I know the anxiety they bring to your soul. But once you have made the commitment to be guided by Me, all anxiety will flee, and you will be free to take the next step. Then peace will flood your heart, and I will carry you to the next level of great blessings I have in store for you.

"Treasure My Word, and I will guide you, encourage you, and build you through My Spirit."

20

EARS ATTUNED

Be alert, My love. Be responsive to My tender voice. Be ready for Me each day with your spiritual ears attuned to My Spirit. As you listen, I will surprise you at a time when you least expect it. I'll share true and great promises with you. I'll show you the "how." Oh, My Love, the returns you will enjoy will exceed any imaginable salary or bonus.

Lazy loafers will collapse in your presence. Rumormongers will be ruined. Those who continually cast blame will be ashamed, for I have made My love, guidance, and My presence available to all who have ears to hear. But some choose to be willfully deaf to My Spirit because they are lazy, rebellious, and constantly wanting their own way.

But not you, My love.

I am implanting strong discernment into your spirit by My Spirit. You will see right through all the arrogance, self-confidence, fads, pretensions, devious schemes, and shabbiness of spirit. Use the discernment I have implanted within you to test the spirits, clear the air, and clean the house.

Observe My Son Jesus. He always kept His ears open to Me. He did nothing I did not tell Him to do. He waited on Me in tenderness—listening and responding. He could see through the masquerading religious pretenders. He could see the wounds of the tenderhearted outcasts. Virtue flowed from Him; demons fled from Him; people flocked to Him.

Keep your ears alert to My tender and sometimes surprising words to your heart. They are more valuable than glistening ingots of gold bullion.

Those who follow their own whims may appear—for a season—to prosper. Yet they will travel nowhere except into a maze of detours and dead-ends. They will race down the road only to discover the bridge is out.

But for you, My Love, every step will bring you closer to glory, grace, beauty, honor, and true wealth because you are making yourself ready each day by tuning your spiritual ears to My Spirit.

Trust, listen, and follow Me to a long, full, prosperous, truly successful life.

"Use the discernment I have implanted within you to test the spirits . . . ."

21

DO NOT CONDEMN YOURSELF

My precious child, don't condemn yourself! I am not accusing you or condemning you. I am merciful and gracious, and I have given you My righteousness because of your faith in Jesus.

I am not angry with you, nor am I disappointed. Don't you know, when I called you to walk in My Spirit I knew the future? I knew of your rebellion before time. I called you anyway; you answered My call.

I will not deal with you as you feel you deserve. I will deal with you tenderly and compassionately. But there are others who will not deal with you according to My character and mercy. That's why you must run into My waiting arms now, and let Me comfort you, strengthen you, and assure you that My compassion will lead you to a bright and rewarding future.

My child, do not run from Me. I live in eternity, but your days on earth are like the grass. You are here for only a season, then—poof—you bloom and die. Many live on earth and leave nothing behind. It's as if they were never here. They lived only for themselves and their selfish pursuits. Do not run from me, for the time is getting very short. The door of My grace will close, and the world will accept its supposed messiah. His reign shall be short lived. But My reign will last throughout eternity.

I made the heavens my throne. I created the angels to carry out My plans. I have instructed them to work arm-in-arm with you on earth as you serve Me and carry out My will. Do not neglect My gift because of self-condemnation. I am not condemning or accusing you. I am correcting and guiding you. Let Me do for you what you cannot do for yourself.

"I will deal with you tenderly and compassionately."

22

DO NOT SETTLE FOR LESS

Why, My child, do you settle for less than My best for you? Why do you simply get by with some of My blessings and not all of them? Why do you remain satisfied with receiving some of My promises but not all of My promises?

When My Son, Jesus, suffered cruelly and died a shameful death, it was horrible and painful beyond description for us. Yet, He went through with it because We had planned it that way before the foundations of the world were established. He did it, and He did not fail in His mission because of the joy that His sacrifice would mean to you.

Even on that torturous cross, Our thoughts were on you. Our only joy came in knowing that We would be reconciled and become close friends, and the door would be open so I could pour out all My many blessings upon you. Our relationship with you is not based on your inconstancy, or the vicissitudes of life, but on what Jesus did for you.

Please, My dear child, do not stop short of My full blessings and all My precious promises to you. Be filled and overflowing with My love, joy, peace, gifts, promotions, authority, and power. Allow My Spirit to lift you to new levels of victory and intimacy.

Our relationship is solid and secure because of the mighty victory wrought by My Son. Now ask of Me, and I will give you an inheritance. Jesus died, and now His last will and testament is in effect for you. You are a joint heir with Him. Jesus rose from the dead, and He is now executor of His own will. He will watch over it to perform it powerfully.

Persevere, My child, and do not give up. Your adversary, who plots to ensnare, steal, kill, and destroy is roaming about making his own malignant plans to block My full blessings from reaching you. Persevere, for I have given you weapons and armor to put your enemy in his much-deserved place. Authority, advancement, and lavish abundance is yours! Yes, yours! Ask, believe, and confess My will and My promises for you.

Do not settle for less.

"Why do you remain satisfied with receiving some of My promises but not all of My promises?"

23

DO NOT FEAR "HOUSE CLEANING"

My beloved one, a long time ago I chose you and crowned you with My anointing and My presence. I poured My heavenly oil over your heart and your head and named you as My friend and servant.

When you face times that seem like spiritual and emotional earthquakes and volcanoes, remember, precious one, that it was I who chose you in the first place. And I will steady you now with My loving and authoritative hand. Yes, I will stick with you and love you forever.

Your enemies seem to surround you. They seek to distract you, and sometimes you've permitted them to do so. Yet, your heart has been focused on My Son and My purposes, even when your emotions have caused you to question yourself. Remember, I am the One who sees deep within the core of your being; I peer into your heart where no others can see.

I am cleaning house. It's in progress at this moment. I am cleaning out the weeds that threaten your garden of fruitfulness. I am sweeping away those who secretly or openly oppose you, hate you, and try to get the best of you. I will preserve you, My precious friend.

I will preserve your family and your honest friends. I will not permit scoundrels to hurt you. No, I will not walk off and leave those I have chosen. I will not withdraw either My holy promises or My covenant. My huge outstretched arms of mercy and favor will rescue you from evil, hidden traps, and hazards.

Fear not my "house cleaning." I am guarding you. I have called you. I have chosen you. No darkness or disaster shall overtake you, for I am your defender and your refuge. You will see My works and rejoice in the morning.

The weeds are coming out. The hirelings will be mowed down like grass, though they are oblivious to their impending judgment. But you, My child, will grow tall in My presence, bearing fruit for years to come. You will surge with strength because you have trusted My Son, and because I have anointed you with My presence and power. You are My friend.

Think on these things, because I have called you, and I will do them.

"No darkness or disaster shall overtake you, for I am your defender and your refuge."

24

ENLARGEMENT

My child, today I will reveal a secret to you; a secret so powerful that it will bring enlargement to your life, peace to your heart, and victory over your enemies.

You have encountered much distress, reports you did not want to hear, situations you did not want to face, and pressures that have overwhelmed your soul. You have, at times, felt as though a swarm of bees was attacking you with one painful sting after another. You deal with one, and another one appears. It's confusing and leaves you weary and overwhelmed.

Now listen, My child, for I am unveiling great mysteries to your heart today. These secrets are not hidden from those I love. Yet many of My beloved ones fail to employ these powerful weapons against the stresses of life. What are these secrets? Here they are:

1. Give thanks to Me, even in your distresses and pressures.

2. Trust My mercy in your "tight" places, when you feel hemmed in and trapped.

3. Speak words of faith, praise, and victory—not words of doubt, fear, complaint, and death.

4. Do not put your trust in man or in governments; trust only in Me.

5. Rest in Jesus Christ, the chief cornerstone, who was rejected, yet now is glorified and ruling from His throne in Heaven.

6. Use His name, His authority, and His power both when you speak and when you act.

7. Call upon Me. Cry out to Me. I will be your strength and your song, and you shall see the swift power of My right hand.

Do these things, My child, and I will extend My mercy, strengthen you, calm you, enlarge you, advance you, promote you, and work tirelessly on your behalf against these distressing issues—against these "bees" that swarm around your soul.

You will live to tell others how the Lord helped you against all human odds, and how He helped you defeat your enemies and bring you to a place of great enlargement and success.

These secrets, My darling child, are yours. And the victory is Mine!

"Do these things, My child, and I will extend My mercy . . . ."

25

SUGAR-TONGUED SEDUCERS

Beware, My beloved child, of sugar-tongued seducers. You have heard that in these present days, as we approach "the hour" of My ingathering, some would depart from the faith, giving heed to seducing spirits. I say to you, as I say to all My precious ones, "Beware!"

Mindless multitudes agitate restlessly as they become more deeply bewitched by the enemy each day. They ignore My calls and My pleas, not discerning the hell-set traps about to spring on them. Countless victims have come under the spell of seducers of every variety. They are squandering the precious life I have given them, selling their future for peanuts, believing they are headed toward security and gain.

But you, My darling one, beware. Shun the seducers. Be ready, alert, and responsive each day to receive My Word and My guidance. Keep your heart and mind from becoming skewed and twisted by the urges and distractions of the roaming defectors and seducers. Ignore their lies, their gossip, and their poisonous sideshows. Do not give heed to the frivolity of fools. That road is a maze of detours that arrives at the dead-end of regret.

Trust My Son Jesus. Listen for My voice. Value My Word far more than earthly pursuits, and I, the Lord, will give you a long, full life garnished with glory and honor. I will give you a good name among angels and men alike. I will bring to you wealth that exceeds anything you can imagine, and you will bless your city and even the nations.

Beware of the devious schemers who have distracted and seduced some of My people. Watch out for the pretentious and showy lives that outwardly seem to be on top of the world, but inwardly are a disaster. Do not allow them to seduce you.

Instead, enjoy the fountain of life from My Word, the joy of My presence through My Spirit, and the peace that passes all understanding from My Son Jesus Christ.

I have ordained you to be strong, diligent, motivated, discerning, and running straight to the finish line. In all you do, be cautious and wary.

"Do not give heed to the frivolity of fools. That road is a maze of detours that arrives at the dead-end of regret."

26

PREPARE TO ADVANCE

My precious child, listen to Me this day, for I have ordained an enlargement for you.

My righteous Son, Jesus, has made you to be counted righteous because He bore your sins, and you have placed your trust in Him. As I have said in times of old, Abraham believed Me; thus, I counted him righteous because of his faith.

Jesus was beaten, bruised, and suffered and died for your sins, your healing, and your peace. He was oppressed and terribly afflicted for your sake, so that you and I might be friends and partners in My wonderful plan. He did no wrong; yet He was led away like a criminal and sentenced to death, so that you could have life and fellowship with Me.

Only in Him shall My plan for you prosper. And you, My dear one, are in Him by your simple, uncomplicated faith—your response to My Word. Now you have an inheritance in Him; therefore, do not settle for less.

Prepare, prepare, prepare! Prepare for advancement and enlargement now. The time has come. It is now. Soon you will be bursting and overflowing with abundance. Enlarge your containers, My child, in preparation. Stretch, lengthen, widen, deepen, and strengthen your position and your storehouses, for the time has come to break forth on all sides in great enlargement and advancement.

Do not be ashamed. Do not be afraid. Your prosperity shall be very great, because you have placed your trust in My righteous Son.

I decree for you enlargement, enlargement, enlargement! I will personally teach you, lead you, guide you, and be merciful to you. I will hold off your enemies as you continue to trust me, and terror shall not come near you. I have decreed enlargement, advancement, and abundance for you, My precious one. Therefore, no plan of the enemy shall succeed against you. This is My blessing and My doing.

Yes, My child, enlargement and advancement are yours by the hand of My righteous Son. Accept My coming enlargement and prepare for it now.

"I have decreed enlargement, advancement and abundance for you . . . ."

27

DO NOT ENVY REBELS

Do not envy evil people who refuse to know Me. Do not emulate their lives or seek to be like them. They are trouble.

Child, I created you to be unique, gifted, and set apart for Me. When you envy those who have chosen the pathway of destruction, do you not realize that you are weakening your own special gifts and talents?

I did not create you for mediocrity—oh no, not at all. I created you with a spirit of excellence, power, and resolve. By looking up to and admiring false "heroes," you injure your own uniqueness and hinder your own special personality.

I have ordained you to walk in wisdom, understanding, and knowledge. I have called forth every kind of riches, both precious and pleasant, to fill your life. When you compare yourself to others and wish to be like them, especially those who walk in rebellion toward My Son Jesus, then you block the stream of those blessings I have invoked for you.

My child, your enemy is subtle. He plots to rob you of your personality, your gifts, and the riches I have mandated for your life. It is he who entices you to keep your thoughts on earthly things and human "heroes." Refuse—with passion—the temptation to compare, follow after, and desire to be like those who have no future.

Beloved, their lips are trouble; their lives are a snare. They will stumble, and their lamp will be snuffed out like a candle.

Do not envy them when they prosper. Soon enough, disaster will strike them down.

I have called you, chosen you, and ordained you to be set apart for Me. Look to Jesus as the author and developer of your faith. Look to My Spirit as the friend who gives and refines those special gifts. Look to Me, My child, as your loving Father. I will bring riches, honor, success, and great treasures into your life—treasures that will endure.

Again, My love, do not envy those rebels whose end is already determined.

"I have ordained you to walk in wisdom, understanding, and knowledge."

28

FALSE PROPHETS

Do not listen to false prophets, My child. They prophesy falsely, sometimes in My name, sometimes in the name of their so-called science, sometimes in their own self-proclaimed expert names. They are liars; if you follow their advice, great complications lie ahead of you because I have not sent them.

They are no better than fortune-tellers, dreamers, magicians, and mediums; I have pronounced condemnation upon all of these. If you insist on heeding their findings, their lies, and their research you will be hurt.

My plans for you are good and not evil. I have given you hope and a great future. Is it easier for you to heed the advice of false prophets than it is to heed My Word? If you seek Me earnestly, I will answer you speedily; you shall know the truth, and the truth shall make you free.

But, My child, you are confused by many reports, all claiming veracity. Yet whose report will you believe? Will you believe My report or the report of those I have not sent?

My heart is broken over these prophets of deceit who have led My people here and there in fear and hopelessness. An awful fate awaits these so-called experts, for I have decreed My judgment upon them. They shall cry, "Lord, Lord, have I not done this and that for you?" And I shall answer, "Depart from Me, ye workers of iniquity."

The love of money is the root of all evil. Because of this very thing, these false prophets have duped and drugged My people into a stupor of fear instead of faith. Yet without faith, it is impossible to please Me. They have fed My people bitterness and poison and said to them, "Don't worry. All is well."

My anger against these prophets shall not abate. I will send a mighty whirlwind against them. They will pay the full penalty for their love of money and the damage done to My people when they seduced their focus from simple faith in Jesus, the Messiah.

Listen only to My true prophets, My beloved. They faithfully proclaim My every Word. My Word is like a fire to purify, sanctify, and heal you. Yes, I sent My Word to heal you.

Do not listen to these false prophets who claim to be wise. I say they are fools. I am your God, My child, and I shall provide you whatever you need as you trust Me.

"Is it easier for you to heed the advice of false prophets than it is to heed My Word?"

29

FILLED WITH HURRY

My child, harken unto My Words this day and you will see a quick turnaround.

You are encumbered with so many things. The "busy-ness" of your life, and the pressures of tomorrow overcome your sense of gratitude. You feel worn out, stressed out, and filled with "hurry" much of the time. Listen, My beloved. I did not create you, or call you, to be in a constant state of over-reaching.

Stop for a moment in the quietness of My peace. Listen to My still, small voice. I am about to teach you something of magnificent value.

I delivered you from a bad life.

I paid the highest possible price—My Son's blood—to bring you out of slavery.

Do you think for a moment I intended for you to come out of one bad life only to enter into another bad life? Do you think I paid your ransom to bring you into a new kind of slavery and bondage? No! I have called you to freshness and confidence and a place in My presence.

I am not impressed by those who are driven by ambitions, over-work, and the endless pursuit of more and more. I do enjoy those who walk in My Spirit, hand-in-hand with me, to accomplish the things on My heart.

You need not linger in the swamp of despair, My child. You need not remain in the chains of fleshly bondage to those who have other priorities and plans for you. You need only to walk with Me, and I will take you to the mountain top and ordain you once again for success and fruitfulness in My Spirit.

I am for you, not against you. I saved you and delivered you even when I knew ahead of time of your struggles and pressures. I am here to build and rebuild your hope, confidence, and effectiveness, while at the same time disgracing your enemy. Your sins have been purged. You are precious to Me.

Walk with Me in a spirit of humility, a sense of expectancy, and a faith that refuses to give up; I will bring you to the mountain top, to My lush island of escape. Then My presence will once again fill you with joy you can barely contain.

"Do you think I paid your ransom to bring you into a new kind of slavery and bondage?"

30

FILTHY DREAMERS

My child, do not look at only what can be seen, but allow Me to lift the curtain so you can see the unseen. Allow Me to unveil the eternal and invisible world to the eyes of your spirit. Then you will understand those things which are pure and holy as well as those things which are motivated by something other than My call, My direction, and My Spirit.

Like the psalmist of old, you get discouraged when you see the wicked prospering and the wayward plotting of envious men. But look beyond the temporal scene, and you will be astonished at what you see in the Spirit.

You need help, My child; I know that and so do you. Know this, I am a good hiding place, and I welcome you to come to Me for the help you need.

Others plot, plan, and connive, but they are wasting time. With unrepentant hearts they scheme, thinking to earn My approval and My blessing, but I will personally put an end to their evil plans. They have become troublemakers. They are obstacles in the pathway of My unfolding plan. Jealousy, covetousness, and pride motivate their words, plans, and actions.

My child, see what's really transpiring, and you will be at peace. Do not evaluate matters based on their activities. Do not retaliate or respond to their foolishness. Look into My perfect Word, and allow Me to enlighten you to the unseen world. Let

Me give you a fresh glimpse into the future. Let the resurrection power of My Son and My Spirit lift you to a new level of understanding and discernment.

Those who give the appearance of having My anointing and My guidance, but are blinded by their selfish sins, shall be confounded, disappointed, and gravely vexed. I will give them space to repent, so do not be discouraged when you see My door of mercy open to them. Those who refuse My merciful opportunity will become like a pile of dry brush soaked in fuel. They will go up in flames. They seduced My people and betrayed them greatly; as a result they shall be mowed down.

But you, My child, I will celebrate. Therefore, look into the other world, and I will show you My help is ever present for you. Those arrogant slanderers don't see the spirit world. If they did, they would know the horsemen of My judgment have already arrived at their doorstep. Be at peace, My child.

They were once a part of My fold. But now they have descended like vultures upon My people, collecting their victims like a squirrel gathering nuts. They walked away from My plan, permitting jealousy, pride, arrogance, envy, and greed to turn them into dreadful, brazen, bloodthirsty wolves.

They appear to worship Me, yet have set up an altar to demons. They have given themselves over to impurity that rots them from the inside out. Only those with true spiritual discernment will smell the foul odor of their sins.

They mock; they lie; they slander. They grab up opportunities to listen to the dark kingdom and proudly say, "The Lord told me," "God spoke to my heart," and "The Spirit is leading me." Ha!

They swallow up little lambs so they can eat well. They praise their own ways and plans; they follow "revelation" from the kingdom of darkness. They wander, but boast of My direction. They are clouds without water. They are not afraid to twist My words just as the father of lies did and still prompts his puppets to do today.

My dear one, these filthy dreamers, filled with self-importance and boasting, have empty souls. They deceive and are being deceived; they fall into ever increasing darkness. I would give them more space to repent, but they have taunted My loyal followers. They have plundered My beloved ones, recklessly grabbing and looting their homes. They have undermined My work, and the infected sores in their souls have already begun to multiply and rot.

Thus, they shall drink the water of My judgment. Soon, they will be the taunted ones. Soon, a harvest of judgment will be upon them. It's on the way; it will come right on time unless they use this short time I have given, in My mercy, to turn back in humility and repentance. Their plans will fall to pieces, but My loyal ones, who treasure and worship My Son Jesus and follow My Word, shall see My love and mercy. My children who walk in truth shall be honored and will advance greatly.

". . . I will show you My help is ever present for you."

31

A GOOD FATHER

My child, I am a good Father with a deep concern for you. You cry to Me for help and I help. Why, My beloved, do you speak as though I am not at work on your behalf? I know what I am doing. I am creating a wonderful future for you because you have trusted in My sacrificed Son whom I raised from the dead.

My Living Word abides in you. Your new life was conceived by Me, planned by Me, and directed by Me. Therefore, you need not fear the storms of life, for I am at work equipping and training you for your glorious future. Everything I do has a purpose.

Reject all hurtful words that do not conform to My Word and My character. Drink deep from My Words that carry the power of life itself; walk daily with the source of life—My Son Jesus. Because He is crowned with the highest honor in all My creation, you also have been crowned and destined for great honor.

Others will trip and fall because they ignore and reject the Exalted One. But you have trusted Him. Therefore, My beloved Child, I am building you into a holy temple fit for the majestic and royal calling I have placed upon you.

Remember, dear one, this world is not your home. Don't get too comfortable. You are a danger to My enemies, so don't be surprised when their ignorance and prejudice issue forth in stinging words and foolish practices. They are instruments of unrighteousness, and will stumble over My Son because they deem Him insignificant.

But you, My child, have accepted and not rejected My Son. Therefore, I am your loving Father who took you from nothing to something.

Yes, I am a good Father who has invited you into a glorious life of adventure. You can trust Me, and know I am orchestrating everything so that it will all work for your good. My child, speak the things your Father speaks.

Snub evil and contrary words. Do not be anxious or intimidated over anything, but keep your heart tuned to the Father who loves you, and who has prepared a table before you. I am a good Father.

"You can trust Me, and know I am orchestrating everything so that it will all work for your good."

32

IGNITING FRESH PASSION

My child, this day I will ignite a fresh passion in your heart and soul if you will take Me at My Word.

There are those who worship Me when it is convenient for them to do so. They say, "God bless you," and "What a blessing," trying to sound holy while denying Me My rightful place. I will not be off in the wings somewhere, like a magic genie, ready to answer their every call. In fact, I will cause their great plans to boomerang and make them a laughingstock. I have no use for their prayers.

Now, My child, listen to your Father with tuned ears, and I will spark that fresh hope and passion to kindle your heart and soul to a blaze, and you will then ignite others.

First, I must be the center of everything you think, say, and do. You must deal with Me as I am, and not as others imagine Me to be.

Second, I am more real than anyone else you know. As you come close to Me, I'll give you an attractiveness that others will unsuccessfully try to duplicate. I'll give you intense revelation, and the time to speak it to multitudes and to people one-on-one.

Third, I do care about sin. While others trivialize sin, you must resist it. Humble yourself by submitting completely to Me. Resist the devil and two important things will happen:

(1) The devil will run from you; (2) I will exalt you, promote you, and lift you up. So purge the junk and let My Spirit clean house. Don't be afraid.

The time has come. It's here! It is time to wake from slumber and be reignited in the things of My purpose. My child, be God-centered, come close to Me; resist your enemy, and allow Me to anoint you with new and greater honor.

I now say, "Fire! Burn, fire, burn! Fire of compassion burn in My child! Fire of passion and hope burn in My child! Fire of revelation burn in My child now!"

It is done, oh yes. It is done!

". . . I must be the center of everything you think, say, and do."

33

HAPPY

Happy, happy, happy! Yes, My child, everyone is crying out to be happy, and I show you the way of genuine happiness. You have heard it said, "Happy are the people whose God is the Lord." Yes, when Jesus is your Lord, and you declare it loud and clear, true happiness begins its journey into and through your life.

You have heard booming voices say that I have not promised happiness, but only inner joy. Ha! Yes, I say Ha! My joy is a result of your obedience, love, and surrender to My Spirit. I have also decreed solemnly for your life to be happy.

Happy are you when you walk in integrity, for there is no duplicity to steal it. Happy are you when you are confessing the Lordship of Jesus, for demons cringe at My Son's name. Happy are you when you refuse to compromise with evil, for compromise drains your life. Happy are you when you are searching out and growing in My principles and precepts, for then false human thoughts shall not penetrate with their ensuing destruction. Happy are you when you ask Me to unfold My wonderful truths to your heart, for wickedness is then driven away.

Happy are you when you walk in the truth and refuse to be deceived. Happy are you when you cry out, "Oh Lord, keep me from lying to myself." Happy are you when you cry out to Me, "Please don't give up on me." Yes, happy are you when you are scorned and insulted for obeying My Word and standing up for righteousness and not compromising with evil.

Be encouraged, My darling child, for I am now reviving you by opening your eyes to a fresh, wonderful truth you had almost forgotten. That truth will stand firm forever! Happy are the people whose God is the Lord Jesus! Believe it and act upon it now.

"Happy are you when you are searching out and growing in My principles and precepts . . . ."

34

I KNOW YOU

My child, I know you better than you know yourself. I know your desire to lead a blameless life and the struggle you have faced. Put your trust—your active trust—in Me. I will keep you away from those things, and those people, that are vile and vulgar. I will come alongside to help you walk in complete integrity, even when you feel you are weak.

Trust not in what is changeable and flimsy; those things lead to evil of all kinds. Trust in My Son Jesus Christ, who is the Way, the Truth, and the Life. Then you shall experience abundant life.

My protective eye is upon you, My little one. You have been concerned about safety and security, and your concern is not without foundation. Yet, I am your safety and security. Trust not in modern "horses and chariots," for they shall fail you, but I will never leave you nor fail you.

Don't allow your heart to be troubled, My precious one. Look not at the things that are seen; look at the things that are unseen. No matter how it appears, I will not let you down.

Read a portion of my inspired Word daily; then you will be kept from deception. Through it, I will give you a deepening discernment and revelation of things to come.

I will judge the proud, the conceited, and all slanderers. I will punish those who have crooked dealings and have acted perversely. At this moment, I am preparing a gift for you while I am preparing to unleash a whirlwind upon those who have presented a false witness and have not dealt with integrity.

Yes, I know your secret faults and weaknesses. My Spirit ferrets them out as you yield to Me. I know what you are, and it doesn't change My love, My plan, or My purpose for your life and calling. I know you better than you know yourself—and I love you anyway.

"Read a portion of my inspired Word daily; then you will be kept from deception."

35

INCREASE

Increase! Increase! This is the hour of your increase. I am snapping chains that have held you back. I am leading you into a mighty action of victory. Listen to Me carefully, My little one, for I am breaking down prison gates that the enemy has erected over the years in your life and in your family. Strongholds are coming down, not by human instrumentation but by the invisible weapons I have put at your disposal through trusting My Son Jesus Christ.

Increase, and again I say increase! Through My Word alone will you see increase, harvest, abundance, multiplication, and an overflowing supply. Aim your heart and set it in perfect confidence toward Me. I cause the wicked one and his cohorts to be stricken silent and helpless.

You shall shout a great shout of triumph over your enemies, because you have put your confidence in Christ. I am at work, My little one, doing mighty things behind the scenes to prepare you for a mighty time of increase. Do not let your heart be discouraged, for I will personally trample down all your foes, even the strongholds in your mind that have settled there from times past.

My decree is for great increase in your life. Now, shout for joy! Praise the Lord your God, who not only decrees it but also shall perform it.

36

INFERIOR RIGHTEOUSNESS

My child, I implore you to steer clear of religious busybodies. They are interested only in form and appearance, and tout themselves as something special. They boast of the credentials of man, thinking this adds to their importance.

Their inferior brand of righteousness is a dead-end street.

But you, My beloved, I have called to enjoy the righteousness that is imputed only by your trust in My Son Jesus Christ. These religious fools, who judge others by their own standards, do not even realize that their self-righteousness is nothing better than dog dung. Their works carry the odor of a garbage dump—a city landfill.

You are like a breath of fresh air in a polluted world. You trust Me. Nonetheless; I want to encourage you in a few areas.

First, be robust and energetic in your obedience. Do not act from duty alone but because you love Me with all your heart and strength. When you respond to My Spirit's prompting, I will give you a fresh, deep energy, and I will work in you to do My will. Ah, that will be a sweet odor in heaven and a great blessing of advancement to you on earth.

Second, My dear one, celebrate My Son all day long every day. In everything you think, say, and do, revel in your Master who will soon arrive on the scene to fashion you into His image and to transform your earthly body into a marvelous, glorified body like His own. Yes, very soon I will send Him to gather My people home.

Third, live your life in a manner that will make Jesus attractive to all. Your life and speech should reflect Jesus' righteousness and glory. Gain people's trust, and do not quit in the face of opposition. Make it clear that you love people; you are on their side. Thus, you will bring them into a true, righteous relationship with Me—not by petty rules and religion—but by simple faith in My Son.

Stay on track, My precious one. Do not allow the nitpicking, gnat-straining, religious judges to keep you from filling the air with praises every day. Do not settle for inferior righteousness. The truly righteous live by faith.

"Your life and speech should reflect Jesus' righteousness and glory."

37

AN INSIDER

My precious one, you are an "insider." Yes, you are one of the "in crowd." All through life, people strive and struggle to be accepted, popular, and wanted. But you have discovered the secret, though it is often veiled by your human reasoning and scattered thoughts.

You have entered into the fullness of My power and presence; it extends over everything in your existence. Oh, the emptiness many others experience by pushing and laboring to impress people for the sake of acceptance. But you have already been accepted through what My Son endured for you when He destroyed the power of sin. You are very popular to those in Heaven's grandstands; even now I hear them all cheering you on as you run the race I've set before you.

Don't tolerate the pressure of striving to be wanted, accepted, or popular. I have always wanted you. I have accepted you because of your faith in My Son. Your sins are forgiven; your slate is clean, and all penalties have been canceled.

You are "in," My child.

You are one of My anointed "insiders."

If you will harken to My voice, and tune out all the mental, spiritual, and material clutter, you will hear Me giving you inside information—revelation! You will know things to come, ways to go, and right paths to take. You are an insider.

Many of My children no longer listen to My "insider's report," thus, they miss out on the action and adventure. Things and feelings, instead of My Spirit and My voice, shape their lives. They become irritable and sometimes even profane. They grope and grab whatever attracts them. They have missed the blessing of being in step as an insider.

Today, My precious child, know for certain that I want you; I accept you; you are a very popular personality among the heavenly host and heavenly family. You have an earthly crowd that also adores you.

So, today remember this: You are in; you are an insider who is anointed and poised for wonderful victory.

"But you have already been accepted through what My Son endured for you when He destroyed the power of sin."

38

KEYS TO SUCCESS AND VICTORY

My child, listen and I will give you important keys to success and victory. Follow these simple rules, and you will attract favor and friends; you will develop astonishing fruitfulness. Honor, promotion, wealth, and advancement will overwhelm you like a torrent when you give heed to My words of instruction.

- Plant seeds. Those who plant no seeds in the spring have no harvest in the fall.

- Never mislead or exploit others. Never.

- Always present a cheerful disposition.

- Don't ramble on and on. Fools are undone by their many words.

- Be diligent in all your work.

- Don't answer a matter before you hear it out. Then listen for My wisdom before speaking up.

- Don't cast blame. By continually blaming and finger pointing, people ruin their lives.

- Never spread rumors. It is a pathway to ruin.

• Hold your tongue, even when you are leaping inside to blurt out your "wisdom" on the matter. Wait to hear My voice.

• Be resolved to finish well. Avoid cheap and shoddy performance of any kind.

• Plan carefully with My guidance. Ask Me, and I will work with you.

• Avoid arrogance and pride. Humble yourself; I will exalt you in due season. Self-importance is a fantasy.

• Be generous. Oh, how I love generosity. Never for a moment permit an "entitlement" mentality.

• Delight in your friendships. Value what is important to your friends.

• Do not promote yourself. Do not try to push your way into a place of prominence.

• Be reliable.

• Be patiently persistent.

• Trust Jesus to bring you plenty, honor, contentment, and advancement.

These are My truths, and they will work for you. The truth I speak today is like an angelic symphony, all parts working together to make harmony for your life. I decree success and victory for you.

39

IRRITATIONS AND FRUSTRATIONS

I know; I know. People frustrate you, irritate you, and disappoint you so many times. And you allow these things to weigh on you, twisting your insides. Listen to Me, My beloved, and you will hear My heart and find peace for your soul.

My Son gave His life in exchange for all who were held hostage. You are one of those. Those who bring you heartache are also in that number. Blessed are the merciful for they shall be shown mercy. Extend mercy to those who are struggling, those who cause you pain, and those who disappoint you. When you do, you will enjoy a release of My mercy over your life and your relationships. Think of the frustrations of My Son Jesus.

Jesus told His disciples repeatedly that He would suffer, die, and rise up from death. Time and time again, He told them. Yet they just wouldn't understand. The team He selected shooed away children, to their Master's dismay. They argued over which one of them was most important, had power struggles, said ridiculous things, misunderstood My Son's words, and failed to follow instructions. They acted like "big shots" to shut down other ministries, and couldn't get their faith to operate in desperate situations. The stakes were high, and Jesus had to depend upon My Spirit to work in these backward, stumbling, bumbling, hardheaded men.

Ah . . . but look! Jesus stuck with them, even when they deserted Him. He knew their hearts were tender, even though their heads were hard. Impetuous Peter preached and 3,000 men came to My Son in one day. Thundering, temperamental John became known as My apostle of love.

Yes, My beloved friend, you get frustrated with people. And people get frustrated and irritated with you too. You need My mercy every day; therefore, offer mercy freely to these dear ones My Son died for. This is My heart; it will bring a new peace deep in your soul.

A call for mercy always stops Me in My tracks. Ask for mercy, freely receive and give it. Oh, I love mercy.

"You need My mercy every day; therefore, offer mercy freely to these dear ones My Son died for."

40

JUDGING OTHERS

Do not step into the enemy's snare, My child. He has carefully and craftily positioned a trap for My people that has corrupted My church—making it fragmented and dysfunctional in many areas. This snare is carefully hidden under the camouflage of so-called spirituality.

What is this trap, My dear one? It is the trap of being critical and judgmental toward others. Who are these who portray themselves as spiritual champions while they judge and criticize My servants? They are the immature and proud. They lack discernment and do not see the snare they are stepping in. They don't know the pain of judgment that snare will bring to their own lives.

I am not speaking about recognizing sin, bad attitudes, or bad behavior. I am speaking of a generally critical attitude. With the same measure you mete, it will be measured back to you. Do not harbor a critical spirit!

My beloved, when My people leave My presence they become insensitive, judgmental, and sometimes bitter. They begin to feel inadequate, distant, and alienated; so they criticize and judge thereby hoping to elevate their own sense of importance. Oh the pain they will suffer when they step into this cleverly devised snare.

When you are tempted to take judgment upon yourself toward another member of My family, stop! Ask yourself the question, "Am I everything I should be?" Ask yourself, "Am I doing all I know to serve Jesus Christ?" Ask the question, "Have I arrived at a high level of perfection before the Lord?"

Child, there is only one person in all of history who has both the inherent and earned right to judge, and that is My Son Jesus, who was judged for the sin of the world.

Do not belittle other's efforts. Do not be quick with criticism. Do not suppose you can do harm to My anointed ones without being hurt yourself. This trap is insidious. Keep far from it, My child, and you will not become a victim of its cruel prison, and this satanic weapon shall not prosper in your life.

Do not step into this enemy snare, and you will not be suddenly ambushed but will walk peacefully through this life.

"Do not suppose you can do harm to My anointed ones without being hurt yourself."

41

LITTLE FOXES

Abide in Me, and let My Word abide in you. Herein am I glorified that you bear much fruit. I know you have desired to be productive and fruitful yet you have resisted My gentle pruning. My child, I only prune for your benefit so that you might come into the abundance I have decreed for your life. You ask, "When have I resisted?" I answer, "In your associations and practices." If you love Me, obey Me.

Allow Me to prune away those things that hinder and weigh you down. Let me remove those weights that slow you down; let me remove those things that seem important but only serve to provide roadblocks to your progress. I am for you, not against you. Trust Me when I do My pruning, cleansing work in you. I am cutting away those unprofitable things and associations so that you may come into greater abundance, and I will be more greatly glorified.

Some sins seem so little. But little "foxes" can spoil the vine. Even as vines exist to bring forth juicy, sweet fruit, so do you, as a branch on the "vine," exist to bring forth fruit. Little branch, abide in the Vine—My Son Jesus. Please remember, no matter how painful the pruning is, I have a very specific purpose in mind—to give you better quality and greater quantity of fruit in abundance.

Let My pruning season drive you to depend on Me. Let Me remove those things that keep you from becoming all I have intended. If a vineyard isn't pruned, it becomes worthless. And you are My precious branch in the Vine. Therefore, trade the unimportant for My best. As you allow Me to trim these hindrances from your life, I will keep you from hazards and infections. I will bring you into a greater abundance than you thought possible.

Abide in My Word; it is My pruning tool. Feed yourself with the nutrients of My Word, and you will bear fruit in season and out—far more and far superior fruit to those who refuse My pruning work.

"Trust Me when I do My pruning, cleansing work in you."

42

SO SIMPLE

You have noticed many times, My dear child, how fickle people attempt to make something of their lives while leaving Me in the shadows. They work hard, with great effort and intensity, but down the road they find their attempts have been futile. You have seen it, and even had a tinge of envy for their lifestyle.

But listen to Me, My beloved child. Whenever people give priority to matters that are outside of My priorities, their dreams become mere illusions. They end up settling for less than My pre-planned best for them. Pursuing self-will, they end up finding only futility, frustration, and emptiness. Their lives become divided instead of multiplied.

They do not see themselves as idolatrous; they will not admit that I am not in first place in their lives. Nonetheless, all their work, ambition, and motivation leads them only to meaninglessness and vexation. Soon they lose interest in the high and holy things on My heart. The excitement they felt for My gifts and promises dies within them.

Too late, they discover all their wasted years. Their scheming and grasping for more comes to an end; their dreams are long gone. Like a fish caught in a net, they see no way out as hard as they try to escape.

But to you I am giving this advance notice to warn you of the sidetracks you must avoid to be fully all you are called to be.

Honor Me. Enjoy Me. Man's life, as precious and beautiful as it may be, is soon over.

As Solomon concluded, "Fear God and do what He tells you." It's so simple, My dear child. Reverence Me. Obey Me. For I have grand designs to fulfill in you and through you. But it cannot be a work of your flesh. It must be a gentle, powerful work of My Spirit.

Yes, I love you, and I long to walk and talk with you in My secret garden where there is an overflowing abundance of fruit and special gifts for you. I want your heart to be bursting with joy—full and overflowing.

Put your full weight upon Jesus; cast all your cares and anxieties on Him, because He cares deeply for you. Avoid illusions and fantasies. Make My priorities the top priorities in your life, and you will bear much fruit wherein I shall be glorified.

"Whenever people give priority to matters that are outside of My priorities, their dreams become mere illusions."

43

ENDLESS MERCY

My child, I have great news for you that you have almost forgotten. The news is this: I have benefits for you—many benefits. Remember My benefits, for I forgive all your sins and heal all your diseases. Yes, I am He who has surrounded you with tender mercies and loving care.

You have felt weak in yourself, but I am infusing My strength into your life as you wait upon Me. Your youth shall be renewed as an eagle's, and I will fill your life with good things from above. Do you think it is difficult for Me to bless you with inexhaustible benefits? Do you think it is hard for Me to seat you in heavenly places with Christ Jesus?

You have been treated unfairly in a particular situation. You know that. Some others know that. Most importantly, I know that. A root of bitterness has sought to establish itself within you for the purpose of destroying you completely by choking out My Word. But My mercy and My grace have been available to you non-stop.

Picture this: I have an endless supply of mercy, grace, and peace for you. When you are unforgiving, when you forget about My benefits, when you listen and believe lies instead of the truth you cannot experience My supply. Now reach, My dear child, into My reservoir that you carry with you daily. Reach in deeply, and pull out My benefits. You will begin to realize that you *are* being lifted from strength to strength.

44

NOT FORGOTTEN

I have not forgotten you, My dear child. My eyes are on you and have been from the beginning of time. My Spirit has not ceased from His gentle work in your life. No My beloved, I have not forgotten you, and I never will.

You have everything to live for. Jesus died for you and was raised from the dead. My Spirit is working in you, on you, and through you. Everything good from My hand and My home is yours—including your wonderful, bright future. I am watching over you.

Yes, you face aggravations, trials of your faith, and even times of stumbling. I know how this makes you feel. But through it all, you have proven your faith is pure and genuine because you have kept going and continued to love by practice. You never saw Me, but you love Me and trust Me.

Oh, yes! Even the holy angels would give anything to be in your shoes! Chosen. Elected. Filled with the Spirit. Anointed. Crowned with the power of My Son through My Spirit. Oh, the victory—the blessed victory that is yours. Laughter, singing, and shouts of joy should rise up in you for the glorious gifts I have bestowed upon you.

Yes, My eyes are on you. I haven't forgotten you. I am the One who started a great work of art in you, and I will finish it. You are a masterpiece in the making.

Therefore, do not slip back into evil patterns—just doing what you feel like doing. You know better. Allow Me to continue to shape you, sand you, paint you, and fashion you after My Son Jesus. It was His sacred blood that bought you.

I haven't forgotten you. I'm still working in you. I am the source of your life, victory, success, and effectiveness.

I have given you a high calling as My instrument of harmony. I have accepted you not rejected you. Remind yourself every day that I am for you not against you. I remember your frame and issue mercy freely.

No, My dear one, I have not forgotten you!

"Allow Me to continue to shape you, sand you, paint you, and fashion you after My Son Jesus."

45

OLD NATURE?

My child, listen to Me. Listen carefully to what I say to you this day. Set these words in your heart by meditating upon them and letting them become a part of you. Listen with all your heart, mind, and soul. You are nobody's slave! I have emancipated you. I have set you free by the precious Blood of My Son.

I know part of you loves to sin. I know you have given in to lusts of the flesh, the pride of life, and the lust of the eyes. Do you think I condemn you and reject you as My child because you have been enticed and ensnared? Never! You long to be a tool in My hands. You desire to be a vessel of honor for My glory. I know that. Yet you have viewed yourself, in certain areas, as a hopeless mess. Nonsense!

The part of you that loves to sin and pulls you into slavery has been crushed by My Son Jesus. That old nature was fatally wounded when My Son died on that cross at Golgotha. Sin will not have dominion over you; you are not under the law but under My grace. Therefore, yield yourself to righteousness. Sin brings death, and I have not ordained you to be a slave to sin. I have not allowed you to be marked for death. Instead, I have decreed your old nature is dead and have declared life for you. I have called you to My good purpose, to be aware of My presence, and alert to My voice.

Do not allow yourself to remain in slavery or bondage in any area. You are free from your old master and alive unto Me through Jesus Christ your Lord. You are free, My child, free now!

> ***"The part of you that loves to sin and pulls you into slavery has been crushed by My Son Jesus."***

46

SOUND THE ALARM

My precious servant and friend, harken unto My voice. The coal from My altar has touched your lips—now speak boldly! I have raised you and sent you for this hour.

Go tell My people that My Son is returning soon, and they must prepare for that glorious meeting. To some it has become like a fairy tale. Yet the time is soon. Time is just about up. The trumpet shall blast, and it will be over faster than a twinkling of an eye in the sunlight. Those who are prepared shall go; those who are not shall be left behind.

Oh My precious one, tell the world My Son is coming on clouds of glory to judge the nations. Tell the Hebrews that Messiah's Second Coming is near, so near. Gather the intercessors to call out to Me for the opening of crusty spiritual eyes and the blasting of concrete hearts. I will work with you, and great signs will follow.

Mockers say, "It won't happen. No one is coming." Fear them not, for they are pious hypocrites who will have their portion with the devil and those who are wicked. Take your stand, My precious servant, in sheer faith based upon My Word, and sound the alarm. Time is just about up.

Tell them not to run to the mountains, but to run to My Son who is rich in mercy to all who call on His Name. Tell them not to scamper away to hide from My coming wrath, but rather to hide under the shadow of the Almighty where their only safety shall be found.

Those who listen to you will not only be rescued, but their families will survive too. Those who refuse the words I give you will end up in the darkness of My holy wrath. They will say, "Things aren't that bad," and "Oh, we can make preparations for our own security." This proud, arrogant bunch who dismiss your words, anointed from My holy altar, shall be led down blind, rubbish-filled alleys—confused and lost.

My wrath will mow down everything in its path.

Speak, speak, speak, My anointed servant; speak My friend! Speak loudly, clearly and certainly. Do not be unclear or ambiguous. Do not cloud over My words. My Son is coming, and you shall see it all. Sound the alarm now, for soon—extremely soon—it will be too late.

"Go tell My people that My Son is returning soon, and they must prepare for that glorious meeting."

47

REST AND RELIANCE

My child, it is time for Me to turn your thoughts and eyes from worthless things and give you real life through My Everlasting Word. Don't try to deceive Me, for I can't be deceived. I know of your shameful ways; I know that you want to obey Me, but your flesh is weak.

Listen! My servant, Paul, had this same struggle. When he discovered—by revelation—that I was not condemning him, he was set free. I renewed his life, as I am renewing your life, with My goodness. Yes, even as I revived Paul, so am I reviving you, My precious saint.

I will be merciful to you, as I have promised, because you have invited Me to teach you good judgment and knowledge concerning My principles. You have received My Son Jesus who purchased for you all that you need for this life and the next.

Dull and stupid people, who delight not in My Word, have sought to put their burdens upon you, saying this and saying that. They know not of what they speak, though they arrogantly claim to know Me. They have dug their own pit and will fall into it, but I have surrounded you with My tender mercies and will restore your joy and health.

Rest in Me, as I rested on the seventh day. Rely on My Son Jesus to bring you through this life safely. I stand firm forever and will make you wiser than all your enemies. My Spirit shall be your constant guide and will sustain you. My Word shall be your map and will not allow you to fall into the traps the wicked one has laid for you.

I have argued your case and won! Therefore, there is now no condemnation on you. Rejoice in that truth; walk in My Spirit; meditate upon My Word, and I shall increase your discernment and peace.

". . . I have surrounded you with My tender mercies and will restore your joy and health."

48

PRAYER HEARD

My precious child, I have heard your prayer; I have listened to your plea. I will never turn away from you—you can count on that. Even when you feel as though you are not able to "break through," I am bending My ear to hear your words and I will answer based upon your faith.

Do not believe the lies of your enemy. Do not trust the changing emotions you feel. Trust only in My Word and in My Son Jesus, and you will certainly see quick answers to your prayers. But if you try to control the situations, manipulate the outcomes, you will enter a wilderness experience and have no real sense of My presence in your life.

I do not reject your pleas, My little one. I have listened, and continue to listen, as you cry out to Me even in your heart. I will appear, and I will rebuild that which sin, and the enemy, has torn apart. I have heard your groaning. Remember the heavens are the work of My hands. You think only of earthly things, but the earth is minuscule compared to the place I am preparing for you.

I am the God of all Creation: the solar systems, the galaxies, the quasars, and My home—which is beyond where the human eye can see. I have looked from heaven to earth. Now, My dear child, look from earth to heaven. My Son Jesus bridged the gap when He died for you and was raised for your justification. There is so much—so much—that you do not know.

Trust Me, I will not cut you down at this point in your life. I will not allow you to perish at the hands of My enemies. I have ordained you to thrive in My presence and to live in My security with My peace. Even when it seems as though multitudes have gathered against you, I will not let you perish. They shall perish and you shall remain.

"Trust only in My Word and in My Son Jesus, and you will certainly see quick answers to your prayers."

49

VENGEANCE

My child, never forget that vengeance belongs to Me.

You have been hurt by lying words from those whom you never meant to harm, only to help. You have been merciful, and thus you will be shown mercy and be blessed as My Son Jesus has promised you.

My glorious justice will come against the evildoers and evil speakers. Penalties will be issued by My own decree.

When My mercy is rejected and refused, I have no alternative. When pride, wickedness, arrogance, and oppression are not washed by My cleansing Word I say, "Fools!" Their iniquities shall return unto their own heads. They boldly claim that I am on their side, yet I see their hearts and know they have not heard My voice, My call, and My offer of a wonderful future in My presence. You will see destruction upon their homes and will know that I have spoken.

To you, My child, and those who have been humble, righteous, sincere, upright, and helpful I say, "You are wise." And wisdom shall bring you rich reward.

I, the Lord God, shall grant you relief from trouble and a marvelous reward for your patience and faith. I will stand up for you, support you, and give unto you a renewed vision coupled with fresh joy. Yes, there shall even be laughter among the wise that have stood the test and withstood the darkness of the enemy.

I am your fortress, your defense, your refuge, and your protection. Oppression will cease shortly; your enemies shall not flourish. I have called upon My select and My elect to work with Me in the Spirit to bring this to a conclusion. You will be refreshed by My power. You will produce much fruit and be filled with vitality, energy, and youthfulness. Then you, and those whom I have called wise, will know I have spoken.

"I will stand up for you, support you, and give unto you a renewed vision coupled with fresh joy."

50

RESCUE

Yes, I will rescue you. Love Me with all of your heart, soul, and strength. Hate evil, eschew wickedness, and I will rescue you, protect you, and shine My light upon you. Furthermore, I will quickly flood your being with overflowing joy.

You shall see a mighty victory and know that it was wrought by My hand and not your hand. Cursed are those who trust in the arm of the flesh and go about making their plans without My counsel. They have no regard for My will, My instructions, or My purposes. Those self important braggarts who falsely proclaim My anointing and My approval of their plots will be suddenly disgraced.

It is My power and holiness that will bring you a mighty victory.

Yes! My righteousness will be revealed; My promise will prove faithful and sure, for I have spoken it.

Therefore, be of good cheer. Shout and sing praises unto your God and Savior. You who love Me, break out in joy for I am faithful and will bring it to pass.

51

THOSE QUICK TO RUN OFF

My anointed one, you trust My Son Jesus, so I will reveal a secret to you. You have wondered why some run off chasing "this" or following "that." They are here then gone. Why is that? I will tell you.

Those who are walking in My truth, trusting My Son, are relaxed, confident, stable, and bold. But those who are riddled with guilt are quick to run off from My flock to follow illusions. Then they make excuses and blame others for their departure.

My dear one, listen carefully.

Do not berate yourself over them. You have carefully tended My flock and never abused my sheep. You have been tenderhearted, even though you never feel like you measure up. I have given you authority and respect. You have worked hard and brought stability and a sense of well-being to My sheep. You have attended to My Word and My revelations. You have encouraged honest people.

But untruthful people fall into their own traps. They leave their Shepherd to follow enticements, attractions, and shepherds infected with malicious intentions and evil.

These who are untruthful and insincere cannot stay where I am worshiped in Spirit and in truth. So fret not, My anointed and called one. When they shipwreck their lives and forfeit their future, they will run to Me for help. And I will bring things to their remembrance that I taught them through you.

Now you, My precious called one, do not fear human opinions. I am your Protector and your Shield. Do not allow your enemy to crush you beneath the dishonest lies of those who run off from My calling. Remember Jonah. He ran; he suffered; then he obeyed Me. Those who run from Me will face hard-core truth, then they will run to Me for help. They will be humbled and hurt, but I will lift them up and heal them.

Now you know why some are so quick to run off.

"Those who are walking in My truth, trusting My Son, are relaxed, confident, stable, and bold."

52

SECRETS TO UNSURPASSED CONTENTMENT

My dear and precious child, harken to Me this day, and I will show you the way to unending satisfaction, contentment, peace of heart, and life-giving energy.

Jesus did not avoid other people's troubles. Instead, He jumped in to help them. Eventually, He took upon Himself the deepest trouble of all—sin! He did this in a public display of My love for you and others who were alienated from the life-giving power of My Spirit.

This is no secret. Through the ages the archenemy has blinded multitudes of souls to this truth. Yet, only those who are willfully blind shall remain in that dark condition. I, the Lord, have shown the Light through My servants, My Spirit, and My Word throughout all time.

You, My precious one, are not in darkness. At times you feel the oppression of darkness, almost as though you are enveloped in it. But I will show you the "secrets" to unending contentment, peace, and energy.

First, know that I have given you the strength to do this. Do not say, "I cannot."

Second, look at the people around you and constantly ask, "How can I help them?" When you help others, you are opening wide a door for My Spirit to come in and help you! What you plant, you will harvest in greater measure.

Third, let My Spirit keep you freshly motivated by filling you with My energy and words. Listen in your heart for His gentle instructions.

Fourth, keep growing, keep learning and moving forward in My Word. Listen to teachers I have anointed and empowered to equip you. Never stop learning. Read My Word often.

Fifth, always refresh those I have called into My work: My ministers, pastors, and teachers—those whom I have touched and anointed to lead My Church on earth. They need your help to carry out the assignments and missions I have given them.

They face powerful enemies, yet they continue to preach Jesus Christ and cause lives to be transformed by My Spirit. They need your help in carrying out My grand assignment. Many speak and do things to hinder My shepherds. But you, My precious one, I instruct to look constantly for ways to refresh My servants and to do it in an unobtrusive fashion. When you do, you will be refreshing your own soul and will reap a marvelous harvest.

These are the "secrets," My child—simple, yet powerful. Listen to My words, act on them, and you will experience a new peace, contentment, and Spirit-filled energy.

53

SHADOW OF THE LORD

You are My heritage, My child, therefore rejoice! You have nothing to be afraid of when you deal justly with others and do what is right. For I, the Lord, have granted you supernatural favor. Along with favor comes My prosperity. You will never regret walking in My Spirit and telling others about My Son Jesus, who died and rose from the dead for them.

Oh, My precious jewel, get ready—get ready! I am about to demonstrate My mighty power through your life. Jesus told you that you would do greater works than even He did, and that day has now arrived! You will see a great deliverance from the schemes of the one that hates you. You will know I rescued you.

Refuse ungodly counsel! Do not envy those who appear to be prospering more than you. Do not be jealous of men and women who appear to have more power, more anointing, more of this, or more of that. I am the Great El Shaddai, and I am more than enough for you. I will treat you with great kindness as you rejoice and act in a just manner. Those who compare themselves, and become competitive, are unwise.

You are in nobody's shadow, except the shadow of the Almighty. By My Spirit, you will never need to lean on the arm of flesh, for I am empowering you with the Spirit of Truth, whom the world cannot receive because it sees Him not. Greater things! Greater works! Greater prosperity! Greater rejoicing!

Greater favor! It is all yours now. Step up. Speak up! Do what is right, and flow in the wonderful stream of the greater things I have *now* provided for you.

"I am about to demonstrate My mighty power through your life."

54

SLOW DOWN

Slow down, My beloved. People who are always in a hurry end up in poverty of spirit, weakness of soul, and eventually sickness of body.

Take time in My Spirit to sit before Me in thanksgiving, praise, and worship, and I will give you simple plans that will lead to authentic prosperity and good health. Yes, I know the beginning to the end, for I am the Alpha and the Omega; I am the beginning and the end.

I have ordained for costly treasure and wealth to be in your home, yet much of it has been missed because of your over busy days. Humble yourself before Me, and I will lift you to victory, riches, and honor.

You have, My child, often felt that everything is up to you. The reason for this is because you feel responsible for far too many things and for too many people. You allow fear to make many of your decisions. However, it is I who not only weighs your heart, but gives you plans, direction, and separates the chaff from the wheat—the necessary and important from the unnecessary and unimportant.

Sit before Me, My darling one. Listen carefully to My words of knowledge. Then work hard, without slothfulness, on those things I reveal to your heart. If you do these things, you will not faint or grow weak. The enemy's ambush will fail miserably, and you will have prosperity of spirit, strength of soul, and healthfulness of body.

My Son Jesus was never in a hurry. He demonstrated both faith and patience. Let Him be your example, and I will be well pleased. You will see the great victory I have ordained for you.

". . . it is I who not only weighs your heart, but gives you plans, direction, and separates the chaff from the wheat . . . ."

55

THE SOUNDS OF CHANGE

"Get ready, get ready, get ready!" says your King. I am sending a chosen angel ahead of you to guard you in all your travels. Pay close attention, My child, and you will not fear the waves of change.

Do not say, "The time is not right; the time has not yet come." Do not make excuses and procrastinate. Behold, now is the time to renew and rebuild. Now is the time for My changes to take place. Now is the time for harvest—a result of the seed you have planted.

Do not miss your harvest. Do not say, "The time has not arrived." Do not continue in those things that hinder the harvest. Rather, focus on what I have spoken and what you've heard of My Spirit, for I am leading the change for a massive harvest, so fear not.

In your mind you say, "Oh no. I just was getting comfortable. I finally got things organized the way I like them." Yet large portions of those "things" have been more of you and less of Me. Now is the time for change, renewal, and advancement in My Spirit.

Because your focus has been on many things that seem good, and many things that seem neutral, your containers have become rusted and weak. Much of what I have poured in has leaked out. You have relied on the arm of flesh, human wisdom, and natural resources rather than My Word, My Spirit, and My Supply. You have feared to totally trust Me.

But the sound of change is in the air.

Honor Me with your whole being. Put My priorities at the top of your list. Lay down your personal ambition, and I will redirect it and transform it into holy, sanctified ambition. Then your little will become much, and your much will become much more. Then I will repair your containers so they will keep the harvest I send. Yes, they will surely overflow. Your plate will be full, your barns will run over, and you will rejoice once again in My Son Jesus.

Beloved, prepare for a great and wonderful change. Drop the excuses. Snuggle close to Me, and let Me give you the tools for an overflowing, "bumper" harvest. Now is the time. Get ready, get ready, get ready!

"Lay down your personal ambition, and I will redirect it and transform it into holy, sanctified ambition."

56

THE SPIRIT OF ANTICHRIST

My child, know this: The spirit of Antichrist is already at work in the world. This mystery of iniquity—the hidden principle of rebellion at work in those who reject My Word—grows and multiplies until it brings sudden destruction on all who despise My Word.

You are not in darkness like others. You are in the light, for you have My Word and My Spirit. You have trusted in the work of My Son Jesus; therefore, you wear the breastplate of righteousness.

Yet soon a strong delusion shall spread over the land, sweeping away many who once trusted Me. Thus, as you have known My will in past times, put on the full armor I have provided you. Continue in My Word, abide in My Word, speak My Word fearlessly. Apostasy begins with the hidden law of rebellion; therefore, do not submit to those words, thoughts, and actions that are contrary to My Word.

Very soon, My beloved, chaos and confusion shall cover the earth. Do not fear evil reports. Do not allow these reports to trouble your heart. Continue in My Word. Listen to My Spirit. Fear not, for I know how to keep you from falling, and how to deliver you from that day of tribulation that shall test the inhabitants of earth.

Do not accept every "prophetic word" someone gives you. Test the spirit, prove all things.

My child, I have sealed you with My Spirit. You need not fear the things that will shortly be unleashed. I have not appointed you unto wrath, but rescue.

Do not fear. Abide in My Word. Continue walking in the Spirit and following Jesus. If you do these things, you will never be confounded, disappointed, or deceived by the spirit of Antichrist which is already at work in many. I have ordained that you will overcome and become a pillar in My Church.

"Continue in My Word, abide in My Word, speak My Word fearlessly."

57

STEWARD

You are a steward of My Message. One day, you will be required to give an account of your stewardship. Do not bury My message. Do not hide My words from others for whom My Son died. Rather, make daily investments of my Word in their lives. But how, you ask?

Take My treasure—the treasure I have entrusted to you—and invest it daily so it will multiply and produce spiritual growth and dividends. Invest My treasure by sharing it with someone each day when I prompt you by My Spirit. Be sensitive to My urging, and I will show you great returns on your investments.

Yes, My dear steward, I have entrusted you with a great treasure. There will be times of contention and struggle that will demand great dedication and energy, but do not fear. I am with you to quicken your mind, empower your spirit, and keep you from harm.

Some use methods that are unworthy of My treasure. They bait their hooks seeking to trap people into taking the treasure of My salvation and My blessings. They use clever arguments and worldly presentations that cheapen My divine message. Do not become a cheap peddler of trinkets of truth. Be a faithful steward, empowered and led by My Spirit, presenting My gospel and My unchanging truth.

Do not use flattery or manipulation to influence the egos of men and women. My Word alone is powerful to do great things in people's lives. Plant My Word. Make divine investments without pretense, verbosity, or insincerity. My treasure is centered in My glory, and as you plant My treasure seeds, you shall see My treasure harvest.

Do not, My precious steward, be concerned with man's wisdom, position, or rank. For the treasure of My Word has the power to penetrate every heart to produce a great return. You need not entice, sell, or motivate. Simply speak the treasure of My Word, here a little, there a little. Do not be stingy with My treasure, and you shall not only share in the growth and dividends of the harvest, you shall hear Me say unto you, "Well done, you have been a good and faithful servant."

"I am with you to quicken your mind, empower your spirit, and keep you from harm."

58

STRENGTH AND CHARACTER

I have promised you strength. Therefore, rejoice and sing praises unto the King Your Lord. Think for a moment, My dear one. Have I ever given you anything to grumble about? Even when I chastise you, it is because of My unfailing love for you. Give thanks and watch My victory overtake you.

Tell others about My miracles and proclaim My greatness. Sing a song unto Me—a song of thanksgiving—and you will quickly find the strength I have promised through My Spirit. Yes, I stand by My covenant, My promises, and My announcements. I have issued a decree to your enemies that they must not hurt or oppress you. Yet these rebels have no respect for My Word; they have no regard for My voice; therefore, I will multiply you in so many ways that your enemies will run in terror as darkness blankets their lives.

Your enemies will see the strength and character in you that were hidden from their eyes before. I will bring you safely through. I shall renew My strength in you. I am pruning and preparing to give you the lands of your enemies, and, even as in times of old, I will bring a harvest to you that others have planted. Yes, a great and mighty harvest is coming to you.

Sing, rejoice, give thanks, and lift up your head for My strength is now, at this very moment, beginning to profusely and steadily pour into your life!

59

YOU ARE IN GOOD HANDS

My precious one, do you want things to work out in your favor? Of course you do. Then trust in Me! Pay close attention to Me and relax. You are in good hands.

Don't try to figure everything out in your mind. Trust Me. Listen for My still, small voice speaking to your heart. I will flood you with My peace, and bring a wonderful blessing to your home. When you listen, I'll keep you from wasting time on wrong turns and bad decisions.

Trust Me, and you will glow with heaven's light more brightly day by day. You won't be filled with regret or become distracted by frivolous pursuits.

Come with Me, My precious one, and dine at My table. Come with Me; oh come because I love you. I've prepared a wonderful banquet for you. Your enemies will envy you because of all the great things I will shower upon you.

Nothing you do can improve on My perfect plan, so why sit there confused and worried? Trust Me. Acknowledge Me, and quit trying to figure it all out.

Analyzing, studying, and inventing options for making things work paralyze those who don't know this secret. But those who trust Me seek only one solution with no other options; so they wait on Me, acknowledge Me, listen for My voice, decide, and then relax knowing I will work things together for their good.

Look at Jesus. Did He seem worried, upset, or indecisive? Certainly not! I was so proud of Him. He trusted Me, knowing that I would exalt Him to My right hand, giving Him authority over heaven and earth. He was your substitute in death and your justification by His resurrection.

Some drink from poison wells by wasting time on over-analysis. But you drink from vibrant, living waters when you trust Me, listen for My voice, make your decision, relax and move on.

Yes, My precious one, things will work in your favor. Now rest. Relax. Sit back in tender worship. Enjoy My presence, and watch Me work on your behalf.

"Trust Me. Listen for My still, small voice speaking to your heart."

60

SECRET STRUGGLES

My dear one, you have permitted "secret things" to bring anguish to your soul. You walk in fear instead of faith in this area. You are afraid that someone will discover your secrets. Child, listen to the King of Glory. It is My prerogative to hide things and to blind others to things.

Do not seek to cover up your secret struggles in times of calling out to Me. That is futile and you know it. Confess your weakness to Me, and you shall then be able to confidently say, "I am strong."

Because of the sacrifices of My Son, it is My good pleasure to cleanse, deliver, and restore you. Trust Jesus, My child, trust Jesus. I sent Him into this world not to condemn but to save, rescue, deliver, and restore. Let My Spirit do His gentle work in you, and know that My mercy is strong and enduring.

I will not overlook unconfessed sins, but when you confess them, I will wash them away and conceal your secret struggles from those who would condemn and ridicule you. Yes, it is My glory to hide the matters that torment you. Call unto Me and be not afraid, and I will answer you and grant you a great vision for your future—a wonderful plan you could not have even thought to ask for.

My child, there is no condemnation for those who are walking in My Son Jesus. However, it becomes a problem when your flesh rules rather than My Spirit. Walk in My Spirit, and you will not fulfill the lusts of your flesh.

I have not come to humiliate you. Humble yourself before Me, and I will exalt you in due season. Don't be afraid to talk with Me about these matters, and I will work on your behalf to mold you into My image. Do not think I am a gossip or slander monger. No, no, no and again I say, "No!"

It is My glory to conceal a matter. It is My joy to extend mercy. It is My delight to forgive all sins and "syndromes" which are confessed. Don't be afraid of Me. I have not given up on you, for I have called you to a holy calling and am working on your behalf, even at this very moment as I speak to your spirit. Listen, My dear one, to your King.

"Because of the sacrifices of My Son, it is My good pleasure to cleanse, deliver, and restore you."

61

THE DAY-TO-DAY ROUTINE

My darling child, this present world, its culture and environment, is set against you. You wake up with thoughts, anxieties, and concerns of this world. You adjust yourself to your culture so that I am crowded out.

This world drags you down to its level of base immaturity, and prevents you from recognizing the wonderful plan for enlargement and abundance I have designed and ordained for you. You think and act just like those who are still in the infant stages of life.

I have called you, darling one, and I have prepared astonishing plans of promotion and advancement for you. But your attention has been fixed upon the cares of this life rather than on Me. As a result, you remain undeveloped, unfulfilled, and unresponsive to My opportunities to promote and advance you.

Look back over the years and ask yourself, "Has there really been any change?" Have not the same patterns appeared over and over again? Have they not brought you to the same dead-end results? Be honest and sincere in considering these questions, remembering that I know your thoughts before you think them.

What are My instructions to you? First, know that I couldn't love you any more than I love you at this very moment. And My instructions are words of love. I have your very best interests in My heart and mind as I give you these words of kindness and wisdom. They are from My heart.

Fix your attention on Me. Place your day-to-day routine upon the altar as a sacrifice to Me. Things that are ordinary, and things that are burdensome, will then become instruments of change and tools of opportunity. You will develop in maturity, and My favor will shine upon you. You will then recognize My work and will respond, bringing you success and fruitfulness. You will experience a fresh adventure of new patterns that work together for your good.

You are precious to Me, My darling child. You are one of my greatest joys. Fix your attention on Me, and enjoy My work on your behalf. Ignore the pressure of this world's culture that can only cause deterioration. Focus on Me, My kingdom, and My favor toward you, and you will see Me forming you, maturing you, and advancing you.

"Fix your attention on Me. Place your day-to-day routine upon the altar as a sacrifice to Me."

62

THE STRUGGLE

Yes, My dear one, you have struggled with your sinful nature. You have struggled to the point where you have almost become cynical as it relates to change. But hear Me; listen to the voice of My Spirit, and I will give you good news.

You were once My enemy because of your wayward ways and your love for the world. Then, you were reconciled to Me by the death of My Son Jesus, and now I live within you and have made available to you blessings that are beyond what you could ever ask or imagine. But still you struggle.

Yet through the death of My Son, the power of your sinful nature was shattered, broken, and fatally wounded. The part of you that loves sin has already been crushed. Now, by faith, you must see your nature as dead and inactive to sin. Now, you must believe and envision the truth—that you are alive unto Me, alert to My voice, and ready to be My instrument through your Lord Jesus Christ.

I have ordained to use you as My powerful tool in these important moments of time. I have called you to My good purposes, and your propensity toward sin need never enslave you again. Sin is deceptive and carries a destructive power. Many times you feel as though you are out of control with your thoughts and words. You walk in the bondage of condemnation, and that leads to a crushing of your faith, your worth, and your outlook for the future.

My dear one, you already know the good news, but when you hear it this time it will begin to sink deeply into your spirit. Here it is: You, My child, have no condemnation awaiting you—none at all. You have been delivered from the relentless grasp of sin, and its control over you is broken because Jesus gave Himself as a sacrifice for you.

Therefore, do not heed the things of your old, broken, sinful nature. Focus instead on the things that please Me. Listen always for the voice and empowerment of My Spirit. Be led by My Spirit, and you will receive My help in all your moments of weakness.

You are ordained to be My powerful instrument, My tool, My friend. This is your good news today, My beloved.

"Be led by My Spirit, and you will receive My help in all your moments of weakness."

63

THUGS

My darling child, call unto Me, and I will answer you. I will show you great things that you don't know. I will open your understanding and grant you revelation concerning those "behind-the-scenes" matters.

Yes, a great mystery will unfold as you seek Me. I will unveil to you many things that are hidden from the proud, arrogant, and those who are "too busy" to enjoy My presence.

I will smile upon you, My darling child, and be your help in confusing and perplexing times. Be confident that I hear your calls, even when your feelings tell you otherwise. Depend on Me. I am full of mercy and bounty. I will show you a beautiful path if you call on Me continually—a path of confidence, joy, strength, and training.

I reveal My secrets to My beloved children who rest in My presence. I will laugh at those spiritual bullies who are crooked in their hearts, who twist My Words and use them to intimidate and accuse My beloved. They are thugs. I will never quit working on your behalf, and I will relentlessly put trouble in the path of those who use My Name only for their own selfish gain. I will pound them with wave after wave of My anger, and blind them with tears of frustration and pain until they come to a place of submission.

You need not fear, for I am working on your behalf. I will reveal My secret plans to you as you consistently call upon Me and sit in My presence. The resurrection power of My Spirit—the same Spirit who raised Jesus from the dead—will infuse you with fresh joy, strength, vision, anointing, and power.

The thugs of life look overpowering, but they are impotent before Me. You and I will laugh together as we watch them blasted and reduced to a pile of rubble in their own generation. Then they will be humbled and will submit to My plan. You will be lifted up and exalted in your generation. Yes, My beloved one, call on Me and a wonderful revelation will be released to your spirit, and fear will flee away.

"Be confident that I hear your calls, even when your feelings tell you otherwise."

64

TRUST

I say trust Me. I have never disappointed you, and I never will. Oh yes, there were times you thought I let you down; there were times you thought I failed to answer you. But listen carefully, My dear one.

When you call out to Me in Spirit and in Truth, I always answer. I never cease to pour out solutions and answers. Yet, on many occasions, you failed to receive My glorious answers.

Three things I want to tell you. First, when you call I always answer. Second, when I answer enemy forces lay strategies to block My response between heaven and earth. Third, when I answer, you must listen in Spirit and Truth.

Think about this when you are in bed, as you travel, and in your quiet places. I will put joy and assurance in your heart.

What is your part, My dear one? First, trust Me to always keep My word. I will neither fail you nor disappoint you. Second, remember to be clothed with the full armor of God that I have freely given you; for you are wrestling with dark, enemy forces who seek to confuse and discourage you and desperately maneuver to block My answers from arriving. Third, listen to My Spirit for the plans, strategies, and direction I am speaking. Then you will hear My solution—your answer.

Do not trust in mere man. Do not trust in the arm of the flesh. Do not trust in systems, although I may instruct you to employ a particular "system" as a tool in bringing My answer. Be open to My instructions, and do as I instruct. Do not remain passive when I speak, but act on My instructions, for I am positioning you for a miracle, My dear one.

Yes, My sheep know My voice. And you know My voice because you are a precious member of My flock. Trust Me.

It is true. I use people, things, places, times, events, and systems. Yet your wholehearted trust must remain in Me. I will not fail you or disappoint you.

Trust Me.

". . . listen to My spirit for the plans, strategies, and direction I am speaking."

65

MYSTERIES UNRAVELED

Listen to this, My beloved.

I have made you a citizen of My Holy City. I do not go back on My promises. I have promised to let you in on the things I am doing so you can prepare and be ready.

But, My child, your ears have grown dull lately. Have they not? Fickle attachments to things of this present world have muted your spiritual ears, but I will wake you from your stupor because of My love for you. Do not shut Me off, like an alarm clock, when I say, "Awake, My beloved." For I have important instructions that will lead you in the pathway of righteousness, honor, and wealth.

Awake, My beloved . . . Awake!

I purchased your liberty and your future with the blood of My own Son Jesus. Now listen carefully, and I'll never keep My secrets from you. I will teach and instruct you so life and success will flow through you like a mighty river, gushing forth riches and refreshment.

I am about to lift a great cloud that has blocked the blazing light of revelation, and held many captive to that which is seen merely in the natural realm. You will laugh. You will sing. You will dance for joy when I unfold My plan to your heart. You will see how much I love you, and how I have longed to bless you with a fresh start and with riches you are not yet able to comprehend.

I am about to pronounce a fresh blessing upon you—a blessing of beauty and bounty. Awake, My beloved. Tune your ears to My Spirit. Your blinding pain, hurt, and frustration will be dissolved, and My revelation will bring to you the blessing and bounty I have promised. You will see that I, your God, am faithful and powerful from every angle.

As you listen to My voice, I'll weed out all that is offensive and guard you against those ungodly opponents. A river of anointing and revelation is on the way; it is aimed at you this very moment. Awake! Listen! Harken! Prepare! Receive! You will hear My secrets and those mysteries will unravel.

You, My beloved, are a citizen of My Holy City, and I have chosen you to walk with Me free from harm, falling, and failing. Let Me teach you, My beloved.

"I am about to pronounce a fresh blessing upon you, a blessing of beauty and bounty."

66

VICTORY OR DEFEAT?

My child, you long for victory in those areas where you feel you have failed. You have cried out to Me, and though I have reminded you of the strength and power you have received from Me, you still feel so utterly weak and frustrated with your progress. Listen to Me, beloved.

I brought the children of Israel out of their bondage to Egypt. Through My Son Jesus, and the power of My Spirit, I brought you out of bondage to sin. Even as the Israelites crossed the Red Sea, you, My dear one, were baptized in My authority. And even as they had lands to conquer inside My promised land, so you have areas to conquer even though you have My glorious promises in Christ available to you.

Listen carefully to My Spirit, beloved. While they were in the wilderness experiencing defeat and failure, the children of Israel were still My people. I did not abandon them. Every experience was designed to bring deeper character and godliness to their lives, even as every experience you face is fashioned to mold you deeper into My Son's image.

Do not condemn yourself. Your enemy, the devil, tries to bring condemnation to your soul for the purpose of driving you away from My tender love and mercies.

Jesus went before you, and victory has already been provided. Jesus conquered and won over sin, the devil, and even the grave.

Far too many of My people give in to the condemnation of the devil and quit the race I've placed before them. They are impatient with Me, impatient with others, and impatient with themselves. However, the walls of Jericho didn't fall to Joshua and the children of Israel on either their first trip around or the second. Mighty Naaman was not healed of leprosy on his first dip in the Jordan, nor was he healed on his second dip. It took seven trips around the wall of Jericho, and seven dips in the Jordan before Joshua and Namaan were victorious.

You, My child, have not been ordained to lapse into defeat. I know your areas of misery this day, and you are My precious child. I have provided your victory, even though you face mountains, raging seas, angry enemies, and unconquered lands. Trust Me and never give up. I have a great testimony of success waiting for you. Shout the victory because, through Jesus, victory is yours!

"Your enemy, the devil, tries to bring condemnation to your soul for the purpose of driving you away from My tender love and mercies."

67

YOUR MIRACLE MOMENT

My child, why do you wait for something to come to you from outside that will supposedly bring you joy, peace, happiness, deliverance, and power? I have already placed them all inside you. I have implanted power within you to do much more than you can ask or imagine.

But you keep looking outward, waiting, hoping that the answer will arrive from a person, a prophet, or an unknown surprise source. Listen to My voice today, and do not let your heart be troubled or hardened. I have placed all the astonishing power of My Spirit inside you.

Love, joy, peace, fruitfulness, creativity, and My anointing are within you. Stir up My wonderful gifts by your faith coupled with action and tenacity. Don't allow these wonderful gifts, purchased by My Son's death and resurrection, to lie dormant—waiting for some miracle moment.

Your miracle moment is NOW.

Yes, I am willing and able to exceed all you can ask or imagine. But, it is according to the power that works in you, not from something outside of you. Stop looking for resources, and look to the Source. I am your source, and I have embedded within you all the resources you need for all the miracles you desire and all the success you can imagine . . . and more.

Would it not be a cruel Master who gives an assignment but not the tools to accomplish it? I am not a cruel taskmaster. I am your loving Father who has called you, anointed you, and equipped you with the wonderful gift of My Spirit, and He lives inside of you!

It's time, it's time! Your miracle moment is now. By faith, unleash the gifts within you, and then you will see great and mighty things outside of you. Feel the flame of My power within you by faith. Fan the flame of My gifts with your obedience to act in faith. Quit being afraid, and trust Me to take you to fresh levels of joy, peace, happiness, and success.

Remember, My dear one, there is a power working in you that is greater than all the powers in the universe. Now activate that power by faith and obedience, and I will show you all those great and mighty things you have dreamed about.

***"Stop looking for resources,
and look to the
Source."***

68

YOUR SECURITY

Harken to My words, My dear one, and know that I AM the shield that surrounds you, and I will continue to be your support. You called upon Me, and I have answered you from My holy mountain.

It seems to you that your enemies have increased and are taking positions against you on all sides. But if I am for you, who can succeed against you? You have faced many attacks and suffered under the arrogant and false words of the wicked. But do not fear, for I am your shield and not one—no, not one—of your attackers shall be victorious over you.

Sleep soundly, for I am your guard and I slumber not. Victory belongs to Me. My blessings are resting on you at this very moment. Do not follow the advice of those who practice wickedness. Do not run with the crowd that rejects My Son. Do not become a mocker of My ways, My people, or My plan, or your way will not succeed, and My blanket of blessings will lift.

Child, in a short time some of your enemies shall be slapped very hard. Others will be smashed. But you, as you harken to My words, will enjoy My victory and will be fruitful and successful in everything you do. My iron scepter is about to sweep swiftly across the land, and the wicked will be smashed like pieces of pottery.

Take refuge in Me, dear one. Do not fear a thousand, or ten thousand, or a hundred thousand who have positioned themselves against you. Do not fear those things the enemy employs to incite terror in your heart. I am your shield, your protector, your provider, your refuge, and your rest.

Sleep well and bask in My peace. I have answered you, and I am the One who enables you to live securely. I have singled you out as My blessed one because of your faith in My Son. I have determined to shine My presence and My peace on you as you harken to My words, for I am the Lord, your shield and security.

"I am your shield, your protector, your provider, your refuge, and your rest."

69

SPIRIT OF HURRY

My child, My precious child.

You come to Me in prayer, then your mind drifts away to the pressing things you feel you must do. I long to bring you into an awareness of My presence in a fresh way and speak with you face-to-face even as I did with My servant Moses. But you move away and rush off to accomplish things that seem more important to you at the moment.

Do you not know that I can release a thousand angels, and speak to scores of people, to help you with those pressing issues? Do you not realize that I can make a way through the wilderness of "things" for you? I can even provide a stream in the middle of the desert! Yes, I can even stop time for you, so you have all the time you need to accomplish all the things I've called you to do. So why not bless your Lord? Why not sit in My presence awhile longer, and let Me enjoy our fellowship with each other?

I am not angry with you. I have extended to you an endless supply of My patience, grace, and mercy. I know and love you.

Sit in My presence awhile longer, and see what I will do for you. I'll drive out enemies. I'll cause your face to glow with My anointing; I'll give you amazing gifts and skills in dealing with people—both those in My kingdom and those who are not yet a part of My family. I will call willing servants to help you. You will have more than enough of everything you need, desire, and dream about.

When you read about My Son Jesus, do you find him hurried and stressed out? Of course you don't. He placed a priority on His time in communion with Me. Whether it was in a garden, on a mountain, or in a quiet valley He chose the perfect thing—time in My presence.

You will complete all your work. Do not fear. I will help you, and you will know it was I, the Lord, who did it. So, let's have fellowship. Let's chat. I want to show you some great and marvelous things that will advance you like a speeding gazelle. Come to Me, and let Me impart fresh vision and peace into your heart.

"I have extended to you an endless supply of My patience, grace, and mercy."

70

BLESSED

Harken to Me, My beloved one. Listen to what My Spirit says to you this day, and you will be blessed with great, overflowing joy.

You have not embraced all the blessings I have predetermined for you. I am lavish in My blessings, but you have refused some of them for fear of what others would think. Why? Isn't that exactly what brought Pontius Pilate to miserable ruin? Fear of people, instead of fear of the Lord, has brought down many men who were once considered great.

Listen My beloved, listen! You bless Me and honor Me when you freely receive My blessings. Have you not read that I take pleasure in the flourishing success of My servants? Yet, for fear of what others would say, you have rejected My lavish and opulent outpouring of love and blessings.

My beloved, I will change you from the inside out if you allow Me to do so. You will be able to freely receive My blessings—even My material blessings. You have blessed many people with words of encouragement when you didn't even know it. You have given, but not allowed Me to give back to you as fully as I desire.

My Son Jesus, when speaking about judgment, criticism, and mercy, said these words, "Give and it shall be given unto you . . . ." His words are spirit and life principles.

What you give will be given back to you in "good measure, pressed down, and running over." I have moved upon men and women to bless you immensely, but you have said in essence, "No thanks."

My beloved, I want to bless you with more than enough of everything for which others work themselves stupid. I want to lavish My gifts upon you without recalling them. Do not run from My blessings. Do not be afraid. I love blessing you, My beloved one. Oh, how I love blessing you.

I am with you. Do not feel guilty because of My blessings; more blessings are on the way. Watch for them, and receive them with thanksgiving not fear or guilt. I so much enjoy seeing you blessed.

"I will change you from the inside out if you allow Me to do so."

71

REMEMBER THE DRILL

Allow Me, the Lord your God, to encourage you today.

You have often been disappointed at what appears to be a failure. You speak to some with the purpose of helping them, and it *seems* as though your words fall fruitlessly to the ground having no effect. But that is only the way it seems, not the way it is.

When you are tempted to be discouraged, and think your words have been rejected—remember the drill.

The anointed words you speak forth are like a drill. My hand, which is My anointing, causes the drill to turn and penetrate hearts, even when you see no noticeable difference in the life of the hearer.

When you have spoken to someone, or to a group of people, never say, "Nothing was accomplished." Do not say, "I have failed." Don't allow the thoughts that you have "bombed out," or "struck out." Don't think or speak those words or words like them.

You see, My precious one, when you have spoken on My behalf, the drill has turned a little more, and the bit has gone a little deeper. It is penetrating, even though it may not yet have hit the heart. Each time you speak on My behalf, My hand turns the drill a little more, and it penetrates a little deeper.

Though your words *appear* unsuccessful they are not. For they are the drill, and My hand turns the drill. When you are tempted to be discouraged, remember the drill. Soon, the drill bit will strike the heart, and I will pour in the life of My Son Jesus. My Word will never come back empty. When you speak, remember the drill!

"Though your words appear unsuccessful, they are not. For they are the drill, and My hand turns the drill."

72

AN EAGLE AND A DOVE

Oh My child, I have good news for you today!

I am causing you to mount up with the wings of both an eagle and a dove. Fresh vision and fresh strength along with fresh peace and gentleness are about to pour into your life and work, My child.

A fresh anointing—something new, something unconventional, something radical, something unblemished—is coming. Yes, it's coming, it's coming, it's coming! A fresh anointing has been determined upon you and your work.

Because you have chosen to wait upon Me, you shall mount up with wings of both an eagle and a dove. You shall be strong, authoritative, and powerful in this fresh anointing—yet gentle as a dove.

From this moment, you have been given the ability to achieve much more in less time. You'll run and not grow weary; you will walk and not faint. You are about to be rewarded openly for seeking Me secretly. I have ordained you to be instrumental in building My spiritual house.

Eye has not seen, nor ear heard what I have prepared for you, My child. Even your own "eye of faith" has not yet seen the magnitude of how I shall use you in these days. You have proclaimed My Son Jesus Christ. You have sought Me secretly.

You have humbled yourself before Me, and now you shall be rewarded openly.

Yes, My child, I have great joy and pleasure in infusing you with this fresh anointing from My Spirit. To whom much is given, much is required; therefore, use this fresh anointing liberally and activate it by faith. My life-giving anointing is in you this moment. Let it flow out of you and into the lives of those who need My healing love.

Yes, My child, you have mounted up with a fresh anointing as that of an eagle and a dove simultaneously. It was My doing, and I am rejoicing in it!

"You'll run and not grow weary; you will walk and not faint."

73

A SHORT, BUT POTENT WORD

My beloved child, listen to Me. I have a short, but memorable, Word for you today.

You are a highly favored servant of Mine.

I will withhold nothing that is good from those who walk uprightly in accordance with My will.

Two areas our enemy attacks:

1. My goodness

2. Your uprightness

Let me settle it for you, My beloved child.

I am good.

Because you have trusted My Son Jesus, you are upright.

That's it!

74

WORDS OF ENCOURAGEMENT

Oh, My anointed child, I wish to speak to you today of so many wonderful promises. Take My words to heart, and you shall prosper.

You will set the pace in reaping a great harvest, if you will set the pace in giving.

You will set the pace in success and growth, if you will set the pace in ministering to and reaching out to others.

If you obey Me, My anointed child, I will grant you much fruit, a perpetual supply, safety, protection, power, peace, and freedom from fear. Yes, as you abide in Jesus, you will be a hundred times more powerful than your strongest enemy. I will drive back your enemies and defeat them to their dismay.

You will not only have an adequate supply, but I will give you a surplus supply as you: (1) are lavish in your giving; (2) minister to My people; (3) reach out to rejected and abandoned souls; (4) obey Me in all your steps.

I am building in you something that is strong and powerful, something that is solid and enduring.

Trust Me in these things, My anointed child, for I will never let you down.

75

GREAT AUTHORITY

My child, I have given you great authority in My Son Jesus, and have made you strong in many areas. I have poured upon you the fresh anointing I promised you. It is an anointing that will not only endure but will grow powerfully and steadily in your life and work.

My promises to you, My child: You shall flourish; you shall be successful and victorious; growth will be the keynote of your life and work. Your enemies will be put down. Those who have risen against you, and rebelled against My anointing on your life, will be pruned away one by one.

I am your refuge, My child. I will rescue you and save you from the hand of those who hope to frighten you. I am the solid rock of protection where you are always welcome and safe from harm.

Many will be amazed at your success—the success that I personally give you. Some will act out in jealousy, and they will not prosper.

I have halted many attacks that were designed against you, My child. Because of your humble trust in Me, I have exalted you; I have become your personal protector.

Continue to honor Me—not only with your lips, My child, but with your whole heart—and I will keep rescuing and protecting you. I will cause great honor to come upon you. You will feel that this honor is undeserved, nonetheless, I have ordained it so take it and thank Me for it. Always be gracious to people, both good and bad alike.

You are under My personal care.

My child, even in your old age, you shall still produce fine fruit in abundance, and you will personally continue to flourish. I will never go back on a promise I have made to you.

Always remember your strength is in the authority of Jesus Christ and continues by abiding in Him and in His Words.

"I will never go back on a promise I have made to you."

76

ROYALTY

You are my servant, dear one. You are royalty with Me and a joint heir with Christ Jesus. You shall bring Me glory!

Yes, you shall restore many in My ways, and I will use you to bring My light to many nations of the world. I have chosen you, dear one. The day will come when even the so-called great ones will stand at attention when you pass by.

I, the Lord your God, shall keep you from all harm.

Through your life I will say to prisoners of darkness, "Come out and be set free!" And they shall come out, be delivered, and become gentle sheep in my pasture.

I am filling you with joy and everlasting gladness. It is I, the Lord, who gives you comfort, strength, encouragement, and joy. What right do you have to fear mortal man who will wither like the grass and disappear? Prison, starvation, lack, poverty, and death are not your fate. For I am the Lord your God, and I have put My words in your mouth and hidden you safely in My hands.

I am the one Who planted the stars in space and molded the earth in the beginning. I am the One who says, "Dear one . . . you are Mine!" Do not allow others to falsely and subtly influence you. You influence them.

I will give you added years of life. As you allow Me to speak through your life and through your lips, I will give you happiness, joy, riches, and achievements equal to that of many men who do not honor Me!

This is your reward for wrapping yourself in Jesus, My son, and for making Him your refuge and high tower of safety. Yes, you are indeed a joint heir with Him. You are royalty, and these are my promises to you, dear one.

"It is I, the Lord, who gives you comfort, strength, encouragement, and joy."

77

ENEMIES COMING TO CHRIST

The Lord your God is guarding you and leading the armies of Heaven. Yes, My love, I am fighting for you, guarding you, and blessing you in everything you do. Please never doubt this.

Your enemies will be terrified of you because of what I am about to do for you. They will be in a panic, trying desperately to figure a way out. But I, your Lord, will prove to be too much for them. Then I will, in My mercy, offer them a road of rescue through Jesus. When they choose the road I have offered, I will be a Father to them; they shall be My children, and you will be enemies no longer.

I have given you the heathen for your inheritance. Open your mouth wide, and I will fill your requests. I will be your strength and courage as you take the land for My Son.

Stay alert. Watch over yourself, so that you don't wander off into teachings that are foreign to Me. Be vigilant. Don't add a word to My Word; don't subtract a word from My Word. In My Word is the power for discernment, faith, and victorious action.

Listen to Me, My child, and people will say of you, "I've never seen anything like this. What a great man of God—so wise, understanding, and powerful." But you will know that it is My wisdom and power behind you all the way. I will give you courage to speak to people about My plan and invite them to participate. Many will accept, and many will reject My plan. Some will reject at first but later accept, so remember to treat them all with respect and kindness. I have given them to you for your inheritance.

I will soon reveal My glory and greatness in this land. So be careful to act exactly as I tell you. When you do, you will see many coming to Me, and I will reward you with a very good life of abundance and bounty.

This is your heritage as My faithful child, and your inheritance as a joint heir with My Son Jesus. You're going to receive largeness, advancement, properties, storehouses, and a great place to live and work. Remember, this all comes from My hand. Stay small in your own sight, and don't forget how all this came about. It was through the love, mercy, and goodness of the Lord your God. Yes, I am guarding and leading you to greatness at this very moment. Trust Me, My child, and do not trust the resources of man.

Do not doubt, for shortly you will see it all begin.

"I will soon reveal My glory and greatness in this land."

78

POWER AND CONFIDENCE

Listen to Me, My child. Common sense can become a barrier against hearing a fresh word from your Lord. Insensitivity to a fresh word from heaven will suffocate the Holy Spirit's ministry in your life.

There are many voices, and I have given you equipment to test the voices to know whether they are Mine. If you delve into both good and evil, the devil will be the one who prevails at the finish. Some voices are enticing, but I have purposed for you to reach a place in My Spirit where you have no other desire but My desire. Other voices will lure you with alien desires and, if unchecked, will choke out My voice that leads you into truth and the way everlasting.

Fear is one of these alien voices. If you are to walk intimately with Me, morbid fear must be removed from your life. Power and confidence in My Word must replace it. The enemy—our enemy—knows *not* your thoughts and fears. *If* you will not let those thoughts out in public, you will be safe.

Your enemy deals in subtleties. I deal in simplicities. Your enemy is shrouded with confusion and "gray" areas. I speak in terms of absolutes. Your enemy's objective is to allow you to profess faith while preventing you from practicing faith.

My Word is your manual for battle. Do not be an unwitting co-conspirator against My Kingdom. Do not be influenced by alien voices that would subtly suggest that you think and act differently than I would have you think and act. Do not permit your enemy to add your "scalp" to his growing collection. Your mind is his chief target. He seeks to cause you to think thoughts contrary to My Word.

Satan has a strategy against you that is rooted in fear. He is attempting to distort and deny my Word. He craves to discredit the testimony I have given you. He drools at the thought of depressing you and destroying your enthusiasm for My work. Further, he would delight in diluting your effectiveness.

Child, you need not prove your identity. You need not pursue what seems sensational—only follow My will, plan, and purpose for your life.

The Blood of My Son is powerful enough to defeat every enemy voice and bring complete victory for you. Your weapons are clear: (1) The Blood of Jesus, (2) The Testimony I gave you, and (3) My Word.

Now, submit to Me. Resist the devil, and he will flee. My residence is within you. Jesus is your Great High Priest. Harken to Him and to the voice of My Spirit. Then you will find grace and mercy in your time of need.

"Resist the devil, and he will flee."

79

SAFE

Yes, My child, I have heard your cries for help. Because you have made Jesus Christ the Lord of your life, I have empowered you, by My Spirit, to endure patiently for the inheritance I have promised. Be filled with joy and thanksgiving, for you have been rescued from the powers of darkness.

I have accepted you just as you are. Now let your roots grow deep into My love and My Word, build your life upon Me. Your faith will grow strong in the Truth, and your achievements will surpass those of all your mockers.

You have been set free from the spiritual powers of this world through your death and rebirth with Christ. You will tell the next generation about the glorious miracles and wondrous deeds of your God. So, set your sights on the realities of My Kingdom. Put your thoughts on the things of Heaven and not the troubling problems of this world. My son, your real life is hidden in Christ Jesus. When He appears shortly, you will share in His glory.

As for those who have opposed you and treated My Word and My precepts with contempt, their lives will end in failure and shame. Terror will consume them. Abandonment will be their lot in life, for they have not recognized Me as the Lord of the Armies of Heaven. They think only on things of this world, imagining Me to be nothing but a myth, even though they honor Me with their lips. I am dispatching a band of destroying angels against their plots and schemes, for I am the Lord of the Armies of Heaven.

Their ways are futile and foolish. Their schemes will become as useless as a helpless scarecrow in the cucumber patch. Yes, they have launched a conspiracy against My anointed—a conspiracy that will boomerang on their heads bringing calamity, shame, disgrace, rejection, and anguish. Yet they laugh and scoff, unaware of the pain they are about to endure. They will ask, "Why is this happening to me?" And I will answer, "Because you have set yourself against Me and against My servant, I have stripped you, shamed you, confused you, and brought grief against you. Oh what sorrow awaits you at the next corner, unless you humbly repent and turn to Me." Yes, anguish and terror will strike them suddenly.

But I do not break My covenant with you who waits for My help. I will never abandon or disappoint you. Your opponents will be disgraced and humiliated, but you will have joy as My spokesman, protection as My anointed child, and peace as you see My plan of rescue in motion.

Yes, I have heard your cries My child. Your inheritance is on the way. Think on heavenly matters, and do not be distracted by the stubbornness of those who think only on things of this world. You are My delight, and you bear My Name. I will take care of you, My child. I'll keep you safe, for I am the Lord of the Armies of Heaven.

80

GOD'S DOCTRINES OR MAN'S PHILOSOPHIES

My darling one, I will be your guide and the strength of your heart. Draw near to Me. As you do, I will put more trust in your heart toward Me. Speak words that are right, for death and life truly are in the power of your tongue.

Speak words that will feed My lambs. Tend My sheep; follow Me; feed My sheep. Don't concern yourself with My plan for other servants of Mine—focus on My plan for you.

Surrender unlawful desires; take up the desire to do My will alone. There is nothing greater or more glorious on earth than My gospel. Don't miss the greatest opportunities by rationalizing and drawing aside from the commitments I have invited you to make. Cultivate a love that refuses to grieve Me.

Count nothing as your own.

I long to give you a purity of life that will bring My manifested power among men, with multitudes being gathered into My Kingdom through your life and service. Don't be disturbed or distracted by anything. Allow Me to consume your life.

Beware of false ideas, notions, philosophies, and plans. I am building My Church, but our enemy is also building his own "church." As he builds his church, he is directing his wrecking crew to destroy My Church. The devil wants to destroy My true Church. He is competing for souls at this very moment. Do not de-emphasize My doctrine by overemphasizing experience. Do not divert from objective doctrine and authentic faith to subjective experiences.

Continue in the exclusive authority of My Word. Trust in the deity of My Son Jesus. Remember, man is totally sinful apart from Jesus, the only true Savior and Lord.

Speak these things. Walk in these things. Hold fast your confession of genuine faith. You are authentic, not phony; you are God-made, not man-made. In both doctrine and teaching, do not mix man-made philosophies with God-made doctrines.

Draw near to Me. I will guide and strengthen you. That is My promise to you.

"Surrender unlawful desires; take up the desire to do My will alone."

81

I HAVE CHOSEN YOU

Listen to Me this day, My child, and I, the Lord your God, will give you wise counsel.

I have chosen you. Over the years your enemies have sought to torment you relentlessly. But I have lifted up three faithful, obedient warriors to constantly intercede in faith for you.

Thus, I will use you and "the three" to break through those enemies like a raging flood. You will say, "God did it," and will praise Me with all your heart. Then you will tell of all the wondrous and miraculous things I have done. As a result, many will come into the faith. They will sing praises to the Name of My Son Jesus.

Yes, your enemies shall be uprooted, ruined, and forgotten. All their evil plots and plans will boomerang.

Friends who stand with you will be rewarded with peace, prosperity, and great success. "The three" shall be honored with My presence and an endless wealth of My blessing. Day after day, more and more will join you until you command a great army that will tell the world of My wonderful love, grace, and mercy. Oh, the precious harvest is ready for reaping.

My counsel to you, My Chosen One, is this:

1. Daily, remember I have chosen you.

2. Daily, sing praises to My Name.

3. Daily, testify of My love, grace, and mercy.

4. Always remember "the three" who are in the shadows. They are working hand in hand with Me to bring you monumental victory through warfare unseen to the natural eye.

5. Fear not as your fame spreads. You are a private person and are not comfortable with too much recognition, but let Me do My work. You simply trust Me and point to the most marvelous work of all, which took place at Calvary when My Son died for the sins of the world.

6. Do not be afraid when you see rugged soldiers defecting from Satan's army to join with you. They will not betray you or turn back.

7. I am granting to you extraordinary favor. People will be unusually kind and generous to you. Accept it as an emblem of My love for you. Do not be embarrassed by My lavish blessings.

This is My counsel today, My child. Walk in it and rejoice in My many blessings.

82

ARROGANT ONES JUDGED

Listen to the Judge and harken to My voice.

They have worn pride like a jeweled necklace and clothed themselves with cruelty.

They scoff at My chosen ones, thinking themselves to be wiser than My anointed ones. They recklessly speak evil, using their words to inflict harm without fearing any judgment or consequences.

They crush tender hearts with arrogant words from their lips, sometimes overtly—other times subtly. Yes, their harmful words strut around the earth, bringing dismay and confusion upon all who drink them in. Their words swagger through the heavens bringing a stench to My nostrils and a foul odor that causes My holy commanders to cringe.

Thinking themselves wise, they have become traitors by their own lips. They view themselves as higher in wisdom than My delegated ones who hear My voice and obey My words.

Oh, they sit at ease with their dreams of the future saying, "I will do it differently and will have greater success because of my deeper insight and higher wisdom."

"Ha," I say, "Ha!"

Absalom saw himself as brilliant, and undermined his own father, My friend and chosen delegate David.

Judas Iscariot saw himself as the most intelligent of all the disciples. Oh yes, he was an example of cleverness.

But did either of these men prosper for long? Their choices, based on their self-brilliance and imagined intelligence, put them on a slippery path that sent them on their way to destruction. They were swept away by unimaginable terrors beyond what you could ever think or will ever know. For those arrogant ones, it would have been better had they never been born.

In their pride and arrogance, they unknowingly abandoned Me as they scoffed at lowly, humble, anointed ones.

But you, My servant and friend, I will guide with My counsel. I will lead you to a glorious destiny, because you have desired Me more than riches and honor. You have chosen to draw near to Me, and to be close by My side, through My Son Jesus. You have longed for the presence of My Spirit. Thus, the riches and honor those arrogant ones have dreamed about, talked about, and thought about, will be yours instead.

I have pronounced it and decreed it, for I am the Great High Judge.

"I will lead you to a glorious destiny . . ."

83

CELEBRATING THE VICTORY

My treasured child, this message is a warning from the One who sits on Heaven's Throne and brings endless encouragement to those who love and honor Him.

Relax now, My dear one, everything is going to be all right. I will pull it all together, because you trust Me.

Yet you must be warned, as I warned you in the past, that shameful imposters will try to infiltrate your circle. They are defectors who have replaced My grace with ungodly license, dragging My glory through the mud. They reject authority and sarcastically joke at things they don't understand. They gripe when they don't get what they want. They talk big and sound important, but they do not take Me seriously.

Filled with jealousy, greed, and rebellion, they grab, grab, grab—constantly snatching for the biggest and best for themselves. They want to consume it all in their own lusts. They flatter people with insincere compliments in order to gain an advantage, thinking it will get them ahead. They infect others with their subtle bellyaching and smooth words. They think only of themselves, and have no true regard for Me, for My people, or for the Church I am building on earth.

My treasure, My child, know this: They have not My Spirit and there is nothing to their manipulating words. You, My child, walk in the mercy of your Master Jesus Christ. Listen for My Spirit's voice inside of you. I will not allow you to be without My discernment, but you must act on it in faith. It will guard you.

Be fresh in celebrating My victory. Be tender with those who are trapped in sin but firm with religious imposters. Shun their selfish, grabbing ways. Be alert and relax in Me, trusting Me to bring you all the mercy and genuine grace you need.

When you trust me and do these things, you will receive great reward, and My Son, your Savior Jesus Christ, will receive glory and honor and praise.

Beware, My child; rest in Me.

"I will not allow you to be without My discernment, but you must act on it in faith."

84

WHAT DO YOU WANT?

You look around and see My abundant blessing on a few of My children and wonder why. Listen to me, My child. It's simple—very simple. The majority of My children overlook it or see it as a mere cliché.

You have not because you ask not.

Have I not instructed My children to open their mouths wide and I will fill them? Yet so many of My dear ones allow timidity to prevent them from asking everything they want from Me. Through Jesus, I have promised when you ask in faith you shall receive. I have done this so you may be full of joy. Still, many do not ask. Instead they strive and lean on their own understanding.

Do you desire a deeper intimacy with Me? Ask!

Do you desire a clear vision for your life? Ask!

Do you desire emotional and intellectual fulfillment? Ask!

Do you desire good things for your life and family? Ask!

What are the desires of your heart, My child? Ask!

Allow Me to lavish you with all My good gifts. Don't hold back in timidity and false humility as many do. Ask big! Don't stop short.

When you ask of Me, I send forth instructions to start the preparations for bringing your request to pass. So, go ahead and make your list in My presence, then present your petitions to Me. I will surely release it to you. If you ask amiss, I will be faithful to tell you. If I need to tweak one of your requests, I'll let you know. Just ask!

Call unto Me, and I will show you great and mighty things that will cause your cup to run over. Yes, yes, yes! I have ordained an overflow especially for you, My child.

Now ask.

"Have I not instructed My children to open their mouths wide, and I will fill them?"

85

YOU ARE A WARRIOR

My little warrior, so often—more times than not—you have seen yourself as weak, especially in those certain areas which you and I both know about. But today is a fresh day. This day, you can change your image.

"Why?" you ask. You can because I have put a warrior's heart inside you—not a heart to war with your brothers and sisters in the faith—but a heart to war in the Spirit against the things that grieve Me. I am the General of the armies of Heaven, and I want you to war against sin, sickness, disease, poverty, demons, injustice, deception, and hatred.

Put on My armor daily, for you are a warrior! You are not the least in My family. You are not the smallest in My army. You are a mighty person of valor and dignity. I did not create you to be knocked around like a golf ball or ping-pong ball.

You are a warrior—one with purpose, design, wisdom, anointing, and power. I have highly favored you, My child. You are not a victim but a victor thanks to My Son Jesus Christ and His eternal victory! Do not lie down and play dead like a possum. Do not bury your head in the sand like an ostrich. Lift up your head, stand up, resist attack, and call the outcome by name. Victory!

Do not be impatient with My work. Do not be impatient with yourself. Do not be impatient with those I love. Do not surrender to those things that grieve My Spirit. You are a warrior, the head and not the tail; you are over and not under.

Clothe yourself with My armor, My righteousness, My Name. Move confidently in faith. I will assure you the victory as you walk not by sight but by faith. You will take the spoils, for the wealth of the wicked is stored up for the just. My warriors will gather it up.

You are not a timid, little, weak one. You are a mighty warrior, for I have said so!

"I will assure you the victory as you walk not by sight but by faith."

86

REAL FAVOR

Oh My darling one, I cherish our times together. Sometimes your thoughts are far off; yet when you come to meet with Me I am delighted. Listen intently to everything I say to you today.

I have anointed you with My tender favor. Do you understand the significance of this? Let Me explain.

When I anointed My servant, Solomon, with My favor, he became wiser and more wealthy than any other king on earth. People from every country came to sit at his feet and listen to his words of wisdom. They brought him valuable gifts as they sat astonished and overwhelmed at his extraordinary wisdom, worship, and organization.

I will intensify the favor I've placed upon you, and you will see how it will attract good things to you. But I have a solemn warning for you, My dear one; listen and take heed.

When Solomon insisted on having his own way, refusing to follow Me intently, his heart drifted far from Me. He gradually walked in other ways. He compromised My will, and finally ended in deception and serving other gods. I removed my favor from Solomon because he removed My commands and instructions from his heart and mind. I no longer held the high place as His loving priority. He refused to obey My decrees and became sloppy and compromised his worship.

Enemies rose against him. Bitter adversaries from near and far plotted against Solomon's kingdom. Selfish rebels began gnawing away at his house and throne. The opulent gifts he enjoyed from the nations ceased to pour in. When he realized his life was almost over, he recognized his error—but it was too late.

My precious one, I am increasing My favor upon you now. Follow Me with all your heart and strength. Do not drift from My love. Keep your simple devotion to My Son Jesus and stay solidly yoked to Him. Other things will vie for your time and affection; they will lead you to other gods. To delight in the blessing of My increased favor, you must love Me with all your heart.

I love you, and want My favor to grow upon your life to bring you all the good things I have planned for you.

"Follow Me with all your heart and strength. Do not drift from My love."

87

I AM ABOUT TO DO SOMETHING

My child, I am about to do something for My chosen people.

Do not be afraid, My precious child—My chosen one—for I will pour water from Heaven to quench your thirst. I will pour out My Spirit upon you, your family, and all who have aligned with you in spirit and in truth. My blessing is upon your children; they will thrive like watered grass—like trees planted by the riverbanks.

You belong to Me, and I will not let you down.

Do not tremble; do not be afraid, for long ago I proclaimed My deliverance and My purposes for you.

I will soon expose the stupidity, ignorance, and arrogance of those who have closed their eyes to My blessing and My anointing upon you. Their minds are shut, and they cannot think normally because of their enmity toward you and toward My hand of blessing that rests upon you. They are poor, deluded fools who feed on trash and ashes, trusting in what cannot help them because they hold fast to, and trust in, their lies and falsehoods.

My beloved, I will expose them as liars and publicly make fools of them. I will cause them to give, receive, and accept bad advice that will serve as an instrument for their undoing, and prove them to be fools.

Who is it that dares raise a hand against My anointed? It is only a deceived fool who believes not in the full consequences of such evil actions. But My right hand will empower you, My beloved, and the fools will be paralyzed with fear as their fortress of lies becomes exposed—never to be hidden again.

You, My love, I have called by name and equipped, and I, the Lord your God, will bring to you hidden gifts, secret riches, and endless treasures which will cause the heavens to rejoice and the earth to shout for joy.

Yet, what sorrow awaits those who have aligned themselves against you. They have raised their hand against their Creator and His anointed. They will neither prosper nor prevail. No, no, no!

Instead, I will scatter your enemies, blow them away like smoke and melt them like wax. They will perish if they do not repent of their foolishness.

But you, My precious one, will rejoice and be glad. You will be filled with joy in My presence.

You possess and enjoy these promises and blessings, not because you are so innocent or intelligent, but because you belong to My Son Jesus Christ and have trusted in the living God. So, go ahead and rejoice!

PART III

PROPHETIC WORDS FOR PASTORS & CHURCH LEADERS

1

FOR THE MINISTER OR LEADER

My child, let me speak to your heart this day, and I will be direct, for I am the Lord who ransomed you.

My Church has entered a new era. The world has passed into a time of preparation for what is to come shortly upon the earth. There is distress and perplexity, but I am not fretting or frantically wondering how it all will turn out. Listen to Me carefully with your inner man; follow My instructions, and I will pour greater honor upon you and upon My Church.

This is a time of purification. Judgment begins first in My house, and I am in the midst of a judgment at this moment. I am assembling those whose hearts are toward Me and pruning those who walk in carnality, arrogance, and craftiness. I am giving you great spiritual discernment for the times just ahead.

There will be those you trusted and believed in who will not discern My purification and will speak against you—some overtly and some covertly—in subtle but strategic ways. They will not discern the lure of seducing spirits. In their ignorance, some will question your leadership. I will expose the hidden motives of their hearts, for I am the Lord that searches the deepest areas of the heart and soul.

During this time of purification, some will disappoint you, and you will be tempted to be hurt. Some who have left their love for My son and have gone after selfish gain will, with their words, tempt you to be discouraged. You will feel like running. You will feel betrayed. You will be tempted to condemn yourself as you have done in the past. You will be tempted to say, "God is through with me and His anointing is no longer resting strongly upon me." But I say to you this day, "Stand firm. Clothe yourself in My full armor." Though some have been seduced and no longer have My interests in their hearts, I am using this time as a purification and pruning for you and for My Church. I am using this time to teach you to act only on My instructions and My Word—NOT on the way you feel.

Your life, and the ministry I have graciously bestowed upon you, will be an example—yes, a shining and holy example—for those I have truly called and anointed. The coming leaders will look at you and see My strength and honor upon you, and they will call on Me for a mantle like the one I have given you.

At this moment, My child, some are whispering; some are plotting; some are exercising no restraint in their words. In their ignorant and evil hearts, they speak of—and rail against—things they know nothing about. They honor Me with their lips, but their hearts have drifted far from Me, so they have no insight into the truth that I am the one who prunes and purifies. They conspire with seducing spirits who suggest that you, My son, are confused and weak. All the while it is I, the Lord, Who is doing these things to bring the purification I promised you.

Son, be strong in My Spirit and pray in the Holy Ghost continually. As you do, I will strengthen you with dignity, power, and sturdiness that can only come from My hand.

You will discover "Absaloms" comforting those who feel slighted. You will find "Hamans" busy at work to destroy you.

You will find, once again, "Jezebels" seeking to control. You will see "Belial's" handiwork, making once useful servants no longer profitable or productive. In our secret times, I will give you point-by-point identifiers, and you will know those who are with you and those whom the enemy is seducing into his dark and destructive strategies.

First, I will give you deep discernment in your spirit and will present to you revelation in our private times together. I will peel away the veil—the mask—and reveal the hidden motives of their hearts.

Second, I will bring confirmation to you in an objective manner through spoken words and honest witnesses. You will, in some cases, feel blindsided and betrayed by some even though I gave you an uneasy spirit in their presence—an uneasy feeling you didn't want to believe.

"Strike the shepherd, scatter the flock," says the devil. This is your enemy's plan as it has been in times past. Words, whispers, innuendos, plots, and secret plans—I will expose them all. I will shame those who have been seduced, and I will humiliate them. If they repent, I will lift them, restore them, and honor them.

My precious child—one with such a tender heart—I have called you, anointed you, and taught you. Whoever attacks you will go down in defeat, and I will use you to display My power to this generation during these tense moments of purification. I have made you the leader and have never withdrawn that calling and assignment. You have been both a witness and a recipient of My love and mercy. You have forgiven others generously, and you have extended mercy and been gracious in your dealings with those who have cried out. Do not believe the suggestions of those who have been seduced.

I am filling you with joy and confidence. I am your protector and will silence every voice that is raised up to accuse you. My son, they are not speaking against you, but they are speaking against My Son Jesus Christ, crucifying Him afresh with their words and their hidden motives.

Continue speaking My Word. Act only on the Truth and not your emotions, and I will prosper you wherever I send you. I am about to flex My mighty right arm of judgment, for I will have a purified and prophetic Church in this day.

"I am your protector and will silence every voice that is raised up to accuse you."

2

A PROPHETIC WARNING TO MY SHEPHERDS

Grievous wolves have entered My flock, not sparing them or you. They speak with sugar-tongued words to draw away and groom disciples after themselves, making them twice the children of hell they themselves are. Beware! Guard My flock fearlessly and courageously. Use the spiritual discernment I have given you freely.

These wolves sneak into the fold, gain acceptance, become involved, and then spring their trap—stirring up trouble, bringing confusion, and presenting their personal notions that are not My thoughts.

Like spiders, they slowly weave their malignant webs, sliding their tentacles into every area of my flock in order to gain and maintain control. With smiling faces and insincere concern, they gain advantage. Full of themselves, they believe they are My leaders, My watchmen. I say, "Ha!" Oh, the deception that has sunk deep into their souls is worse than a disease.

They see themselves as spiritual skyscrapers. I laugh, for I see them as shabby, run-down huts infested with all manner of stinging, demonic insects, slimy reptiles, serpents, and scorpions. But they have chosen this for themselves.

They are spots in your assembly and clouds without water. They are contentious in their character and overflowing with self-righteousness. They are whitewashed tombs.

These false ones have tried to make Me fit their own fashion and deny My sovereign right to their lives. They pray with verbosity, but I don't listen. They are deceived, and because they are deceived they deceive those who willingly or unwittingly come under their controlling influence.

They speak evil of dignitaries and authorities, not knowing the penalty they will share in the end. They criticize the weak and the poor and never defend my anointed ones. They stagger under religious baggage, while outwardly shining and giving the appearance of godliness. No, they are not like Me. They do not represent Me. They do not speak for Me, for they do not honor Me or My ways.

Insensitive to My Spirit, presumptuous in their attitudes and words, they possess an enormous capacity to justify their thoughts and actions and set themselves up as authorities, but they deny Me My rightful place as their Creator. They crow, "Lord, Lord." It makes me want to spew them out permanently. Their hypocrisy nauseates me.

They are outwardly unreasonable and demanding. Because they have ignored My repeated call to their hearts, inwardly they have become withered, fruitless gardens—brown and useless. They are ego-filled to the brim. They offer no mercy to their victims and no tenderness to the bruised.

Imaginations, suspicions, and mythical conjecture dominate their thoughts. Some souls who have followed their influence have already arrived in hell. They are now confined in the habitat of the damned, awaiting My Great White Throne of Judgment.

They speak of My Son Jesus, especially when it is to their advantage. Yet, they have not submitted to My Son, or to His words. Neither have they submitted to My Spirit. I will not always strive with them. Their pride has caused a stench to reach into the heavens.

Court them not, dear overseer. Court them not for friendship. Court them not for money. Seek them not for their prayers. I no longer listen to their prayers. As I instructed My servant, Jeremiah, "Pray no more for these people. They have gone too far."

Compromise not with their plans and suggestions, for you will surely suffer awful consequences if you do. Place them not into the positions they seek. If you don't harken unto Me, you will, after a short time, shake your head and ask, "Why didn't I listen to the Lord instead of them?"

They are betrayers, deceivers, and spiritual abusers.

They are full of themselves, and have been at cross-purposes with My will and My plans for too long now. They are on their last leg at this moment, but they don't see what's coming.

Their time is short now. I am about to launch waves of my severity over these incessant destroyers. They are like their father—all of them. They are hell-bound, but they don't believe it. Oh, I hate their pride. I don't even listen to their prayers anymore. They stink to Heaven. I have determined to hear only one prayer from them, and that is a prayer begging for mercy and My forgiveness for the devastation they have left in their wake, and for serving another god, who is not a god at all but an evil principality called mammon.

Their inflated heads are about to deflate like punctured balloons. There will be no place for them to run, no place to hide from My severe judgment. They are now on their last legs; they are at their final opportunity to repent. Doom is looming over their souls at this moment and over their children and their children's children. But even as hard-hearted fools rejected My prophets of old, likewise some of these insensitive, closed-hearted simpletons will reject My final offer and suffer horrors they thought they would never see.

They will say critically and arrogantly, "Look at this word. Look at this mistake. This imperfect message cannot be from the Lord." That is what their nature has become. They look for reasons not to believe, rather than to simply trust in Me.

They have terrorized My precious servants, My anointed ones. Now disaster is on the way, unless they sincerely cry out for My mercy in genuine repentance.

They are spiritually cheap and shabby. That's how I see them. They think they smell like fragrant perfume, but in reality they smell like rotting cabbage.

My dear overseer! How I long to protect you and the flock over which I have given you care. But you must give heed to what My Spirit is saying. Make no delay in dealing firmly with these misfits in disguise, these wolves who wear sheep's clothing. Do not fear them when you act courageously against these false leaders.

A firestorm of judgment will shortly be loosed upon them. And all those who rally on their behalf and have come under their bewitching spell shall come to the same fate—unless they too repent and cry out for My mercy. Oh, I love to give mercy.

These filthy seducers see themselves as roses in My garden; I see them as trampled patches of weeds, thistles, and thorns with no beauty or fragrance in their spirits or souls. The only thing they have done with My work is to hinder it, while pretending to advance it. Many times, they have deliberately missed My visitation to My precious people. Hell will soon swallow them and those who follow them.

[illegible]cause of their deceiving works and words, and their high self-[illegible]ion, they have chosen a curse.

"But why do they seem to prosper?" you wonder. I answer, "Through witchcraft and pagan practices." Although they deny it with fierce intensity, I assure you that mammon is their pagan god.

Their souls atrophied years ago, because they chose darkness over light and self-will over My will. Now darkness and trouble will pursue them; goodness and mercy will pursue you, My precious overseer.

They have become blindfolded blockheads who no longer have any clue concerning My will and purposes.

Now, My dear overseer—called and anointed—you must occupy My Word so I can give you deep discernment and wisdom. I am with you; I am preparing to advance you. You must protect My flock from the false brethren that would abuse and seek to harm them.

Keep lifting up My Son Jesus Christ, and keep Him central in everything you do.

A bright future awaits you if you stand strong in guarding the souls I have sent to be under your watchful care. I am with you now. I will stand with you always. Because you have humbled yourself before Me, I will exalt you. The people will know, without doubt, that I have handpicked you for this hour.

3

A PROPHETIC WORD TO CHURCH LEADERS

This prophetic word came to me during a time of stagnation in the church

My Church, My Church! I ordained you to be a city set on a hill, one that cannot be hidden. I cared for you. I guided you and instructed you along the way. I held your hand as a father holds the hand of his child as they stroll together through a peaceful park.

You walked with Me, fervent in prayer, doing everything I instructed. I blessed you and made you stunningly beautiful.

You advanced My Word through your teachings. You set in motion many ministries to assist people. You helped My missionary servants carry My Word to far away countries. As I promised, I made you a blessing to many nations of the world and to many ethnic groups.

Nonetheless, now—in this critical moment—you stand to lose your place in history, and it's all because of nonsense.

There is something I must address to My leaders.

I send you this solemn warning because time is about up. When I called you to advance, you often retreated down an easier path. I called you, equipped you, and appointed you to be steady and solid as a disciple-making community for the many ethnic groups in the surrounding areas.

I announced to you, years ago, that I would establish a great, anointed, Spirit-filled church in every region of your country. I chose *you* to be one of those churches.

However, now you are poised to sit in the shadows. Unless you repent now, and order your priorities afresh, I will send another obedient, hard-working servant to come on the scene and take over your city, your county, your area, and your place. I must send him because he will obey my plan. But if you will hear My voice this day and give heed to it, I will send him to another city, leaving you to carry out My plans and strategies. You will be restored to the position of greatness to which I originally called you; I will add even more splendor, dignity, and fruitfulness to you.

If you heed My call now, I will advance you at an accelerated pace and bless and prosper each of those who harken to My voice. If you do not heed My call, I will still love you and use you in a limited fashion, but I will no longer be able to lift you to the magnificence I intended.

You are behind schedule. Yes, you are lagging years behind where I commissioned you to be. You are behind schedule because of the nonsense of leaders who lust and loaf, lavishly wasting time, energy, and money on those things that do not profit.

Even now, those in rebellion—those who can't even discern My voice anymore—are developing their thesis-like excuses, which I, the Lord your God, am tired of hearing. Oh yes, they always have a reason. I will not listen to them or their human justifications any longer.

I spoke to you years ago. I told you that if you disobeyed My voice I would cause you to reel to and fro and never rise to the glory and majesty to which I called you. I warned you that confusion would come upon you if you disobeyed Me and that you would become disoriented and weak. At that time, you boldly obeyed Me; you took Me at My word. Even though it was a painful season, you obeyed and did not make excuses by spouting self-justifying reasons for taking the easy way. I rewarded you greatly with increase and growth, and I lavished bountiful blessings upon you as you chose My way, even when it appeared to be the "hard" path.

You heeded My warning then, and prospered spiritually like no other in the history of this entire region. I advanced you, promoted you, and crowned you with My glorious anointing. I will do the same again, if you will heed My warning.

The shepherd will speak, and those who are not heeding My words and warnings will become agitated, insulted, and quickly offended. They will think evil thoughts of rebellion, and you will notice their fruit withering. Of necessity, I must prune some, but don't be afraid My Church, don't be afraid of My pruning.

Now . . . there are issues I am compelled to bring up to the leadership of My precious Church. Fear not, for I warn you in advance that even some from your own ranks will dismiss this message and say it is manipulative and not from Me. "Ha!" I say. I raised a simple shepherd from the common people and gave him a prophetic anointing with words from My heart and fire from My altar.

Some will dismiss My prophet, offering myriads of so-called reasons. But the consequences of dismissing My warning shall be serious—very serious. I am the Lord; I am building My Church.

What have I seen in My Church leaders? What have I, the Lord, observed? I will lay it before you now.

In many, I have seen a deep sincerity and a genuine heart of worship. In some, I have observed a speedy obedience and submission to My will. I have seen concern for My purposes and My intentions. I have seen deep compassion for the bruised and wounded—particularly those wounded by false shepherds. I have seen love for people in many of the servant-leaders in My Church—a love that is not only talked about, but also put into practical action.

Yet, My beloved Church, I have also had to turn My face from you because of leaders who no longer serve My purposes—leaders enslaved to lusts which become increasingly insatiable. Leeches of lust grip their souls, and all the while they spout, "God told me this, God showed me that, God did this for me. I am closer to God than ever."

I have observed others, from your very own ranks, who have a different agenda. In their darkness, they affirm it as My agenda, but I tell you it is not.

In others, I have recognized posturing, pride, laziness, fuzzy focus, and the cursed desire for earthly security—which is like a debilitating disease in the body of My leadership. Oh My Church! How I long to take you under My wing, and under My shadow, to protect you from what is ahead. Yet, I can only do so when you return to Me with a repentant heart and a commitment to fully obey My voice and My Word. You must follow Me not what you perceive to be the easy road.

Some of My leaders have a deep love for other things that have gobbled up all the space in their hearts. They no longer hunger or have room for Me there. Instead, they have become obsessed with appearances. They are indifferent to others and busy with everything else while not really caring about or doing their assigned jobs. They love music that feeds their ego, rather than worshiping and singing to bless Me. They think they are superior; they think themselves to be safe and secure, trusting their "stuff" instead of the Living God who loves them and longs to lavish on them everything they ever dreamed of and more. Their focus is now darkened by desires and cares for other things that will never satisfy.

My Church, My Church! Unless you repent and return to Me with your whole heart, you will trade your glory for shame; you will wander in the dark and stumble upon nothing but a dead-end street.

Soon it will be too late. Distress, anguish, and darkness will soon blanket the earth. Time is about up. I must lift up strong and able leaders to replace the self-obsessed shepherds who refuse My revelation. If My leaders repent, however, I will raise up strong, able leaders to serve under them, and not from the outside. When you turn to Me wholeheartedly, you will receive honor. You will be filled with My glory—splendid in the land—and will glow like the stars with My anointing.

Those pursuing another agenda have hindered My true servant-leaders. They have created staleness and a slow down. Those who have followed any agenda except Mine will receive My mercy, restoration, and advancement only when they return *now* with raw repentance.

I desire My life-giving Spirit to be on each servant-leader. I want each of My servant-leaders to speak powerful, prophetic words that penetrate the hearts of their hearers. I want to be their delight and joy once again.

If you follow only My agenda and turn from things that profit not, I will make you glorious. Nations of souls will come to you—yes, they will come to you. I will look out for you. I will be your safe hiding place, and you will be secure, blessed, and bountifully prosperous. I will give you new, unheard of spurts of growth. You will become brilliant leaders who will triumph over every foe. You will be strong and seize many new territories for Me. I promise you for I am your Lord, your Father, and your God.

Time is about up!

My Son Jesus is coming, and My Church is not ready. It is unprepared because of the *few* who hold tenaciously to their misplaced priorities. They hold back the throttle for everyone, even as disgraceful Achan caused defeat for all of Israel because of his stubborn refusal to let go of cursed things. He and his family lost everything, including their lives, for hindering My people and stopping the advancement of My agenda.

Now, listen to Me! I am serious—very serious.

When clear, unrefined repentance comes, I'll be right there in My mercy to comfort, restore, and release My fresh, concentrated anointing. It will be obvious and apparent to all who love and honor Me.

Those who remain unrepentant shall be exposed and dismissed from My plan because they chose unprofitable nonsense over My unrelenting mandate.

Already, My intercessors are calling on Me to purge those who, in their careless pride, follow a false agenda. I am tired of the comfortable loafers who care more about payday than they do about people. Even at this moment, there is one who is rebelling in heart and thinking about making excuses. But all excuses are now exhausted.

Time is about up!

I must now have a glowing witness in this region, a strong and powerful witness to exhibit My tireless love for sinners. I must have a witness to extend My arms of mercy and grace toward the wounded, abandoned, and rejected. I must have servant-leaders as witnesses, clean and being changed daily, to lift up My Son Jesus Christ. They must tell people that Jesus died and rose for them. I must have witnesses to roll up their sleeves; they must get down in the dirt and establish many disciples before it is too late.

Oh My Church, My Church! My heart has been heavy over your sluggishness. Some leaders are proud of where they are now, but I say you are not even one-eighth of where I commissioned you to be. So erase your pride and come humbly before Me; let Me lift you up.

You have been like a snail when I called you to be like a swift and graceful horse.

Some say, "Oh, but I have to do my paperwork." I say, "Yes, but don't neglect the people for your paperwork." My Son died for people not for paper. Some say, "Oh, but this and that," as they insert their own flimsy rationalizations. But I say, "If you harken to *this* word from My heart, the end result will be an enormous miracle blessing for both you and your followers."

Some leaders have missed immense personal blessings and miracles because they were "too busy" to hear and heed My voice. The result? They have lost wealth, have withered relationships and vanished time. Now they are dried up, stunted, and going backward.

I call My chosen leaders to be dependable and loyal. I call My chosen leaders to be passionate about My Son and compassionate with My people. I call My chosen leaders to express kindness, even to those who might seem unworthy of My grace. I call My chosen leaders to be quick to repent as soon as I point out a misstep or site of disobedience.

I will no longer tolerate self-important, isolated, arrogant leaders who are, in reality, spiritually withered in My vineyard. Emptiness and desolation shall be pronounced upon them. They love paydays, and payday will come to them. But it won't be the payday they expect. It will be a jarring payday for their laziness, lethargy, and abuse. They will take their pay; but afterward, they will emerge stagnant and stinky—others will shudder to be around them.

Danger is just ahead for all leaders who no longer seek My face but continue in complacent loafing, boastful pride, or obsessive lust, all the while maintaining the attitude, "all is well." That attitude disgusts Me. Following fantasy rather than My vision is lethal and will be exposed.

But wait! You are wounded because of some, but it is not a fatal wound. You are not past the point of no return. If you turn to Me with all your heart, and do not resist My housecleaning, you'll be restored and promoted to a position greater than before.

Oh My Church! Make your home in Me again. Call My leaders to a holy convocation for prayer, fasting, and reflection. Listen to My revelation with your spirit and meditate upon it and take action. Not the hearers, but the doers will be justified. You will be revered as My anointed ones, you will be honored and respected all over the world.

Weak, sickly harvests will become bumper crops, and your barns will overflow. Deny your own agenda and embrace Mine. Don't bankrupt your future with contaminated worship. Don't hold back in timidity and fear. You have nothing to fear by following My will and strategies. I have planned to fill you, My Church, with a glory and splendor that is seldom seen or experienced.

Get going now, My Church. Move ahead, My chosen servant-leaders. I will be with you, advancing you, shielding you, and giving you everything you need for a great and mighty harvest. Those who are willing to actively follow My agenda and strategies will never be thrown into confusion and dismantlement, as others will be who refuse My voice.

Now is the time to get moving. Why? Because time is almost up. You are not ignorant of these things; now is the time!

"I call my chosen leaders to be dependable and loyal."

4

For the Pastor

MY CHOSEN SHEPHERD

A Word for the Shepherd I Have Chosen

You, my darling child, are the shepherd I have chosen for My purposes in this city. My special favor is upon you. I started this work, and I will finish it, for I am Lord of the Church. I have ordained a crown of beauty to be placed upon My work in this city. Harken to Me this day, and drink My words deeply into your spirit for they will refresh and revive you.

At this very hour, I am preparing something beyond what you have seen in the past. I am laying the groundwork now. Do not walk in fear and anxiety, but know My hand is upon you, this church, this city, and this new thing I am preparing.

I am calling and commissioning true intercessors—watchmen—who will call forth what I have already decreed. My Spirit is choosing them now, and their hearts are already beginning to recognize My call. Yes, I have decreed a new and holy thing. But it has been hindered by hidden foes. My commissioned watchmen shall call to release support forces from my armies, and the darkness shall not prevail.

What is coming, you ask?

I will give you a glimpse, My shepherd. A refreshing and flourishing time in My Spirit is just ahead. Abundant prosperity will flow to those who have walked humbly and obediently before Me. I am releasing, at the request and decree of My watchmen, increased power to achieve all I have spoken in word, vision, and prophecy.

A filling of My glory will soon burst upon you. Do not be intimidated by those who have chosen evil and crooked paths, for their plans will quickly, without warning, be destroyed.

But for you, My shepherd, the one who has longed to feed My people with knowledge and wisdom, and for My Church, expect. . .

. . . a rebuilding

. . . a reviving

. . . a double portion of honor

. . . a double portion of wealth

At precisely the right moment, I will call it forth, and it shall be exactly as I have spoken. You will not lift a hand to bring this to pass. I have spoken it, the watchmen shall decree it, and surely it shall break forth upon you like an unstoppable flood from Heaven.

My favor is toward you and on you. Your honor, and the honor of My Church, will blaze like a burning torch amidst the darkness. I am holding you in My hand, sustaining you with My Word, prospering you with My promises, and strengthening you in faith through My Word and My Spirit.

Praise shall be on the lips of all who enter My Sanctuary.

Whispering, backbiting, and all evil speaking shall be judged. My severe anger is now unleashed against all who arrogantly whisper or plot against you. Humiliation and shame shall cover all who have whispered against My anointed. Without holy repentance, and a return to their first love, they shall never rise or truly succeed. They have made their own plans for success—their own dreams and goals—but they have planted evil seeds and must reap an evil harvest in their own future.

Nothing they attempt will be productive for they have chosen the way of Cain, Balaam, and Absalom. When success seems to appear for them, it will be only for a brief moment; then an evil tide will strike, and they will see that their work was all in vain. They must drink the bitter wine they have pressed for others. Oh, how I long for them to return that I may cancel the charges and reverse their fate so that all their labors be not in vain.

But you, My shepherd, and the ones you lead in My Word, shall see a new day dawn.

Lost sheep will soon be coming home. Entire families and ethnic groups will come in response to your beacon.

Authorities will arrive from near and far to view firsthand your brilliant radiance. Yes, My Temple shall be glorious and filled with splendor. My watchmen shall call it forth by My will and for My purposes.

Wealth and riches will pour forth into your treasuries and storehouses. I have declared it, and I have ordered it. Yes, I am the rewarder, and I will reward the watchmen, the shepherd, the true prophet, and those who follow the beacon I have lit in you.

Oh shepherd, continue to unlock My Word to the people I am sending you. Never cease to point them to My Son Jesus

Christ, who is the true and living Lord. I have given you a new crown of beauty which will begin to attract tens of thousands in this land, and many more in other lands. Do not be afraid of this special favor and the new thing that I have ordained.

My watchmen, your spiritual guards, are calling on Me now, and I will do it.

And though I am using you as My shining instrument, you will not become proud because you know it was My anointed watchmen who called and decreed this new thing, and it was My power that brought it to pass.

Oh shepherd, prepare for these things that I have unveiled; rejoice, for I have spoken . . . and I will do it.

"Never cease to point them to My Son, Jesus Christ, who is the true and living Lord."

PART IV
FINAL THOUGHTS

Behold, I stand at the door, and knock:
if any man hear my voice, and open
the door, I will come in to him,
and will sup with him,
and he with me.
—Revelation 3:20

FINAL THOUGHTS

Do you see it now?

Do you really see it?

Can you see the "Private Garden" with your eyes of faith?

Can you hear the heart-warming words of the Father who loves you and embraces you?

Are you receiving tender words from heaven to encourage you, bless you, and strengthen you? God longs to meet with you daily in your personal private garden where He will intimately reveal practical, functional, life-giving words that will give your life the winning edge.

You can step into your own private garden anytime, anywhere. You will be refreshed, educated, and equipped. When you enter your private garden you bring a deeply satisfying smile to your Creator's face while your own heart becomes flooded with reassuring prophetic words from God's heart.

The prophetic words I have shared in this book were deposited in my soul during my times of worship, Bible reading, and prayer while in my own personal private garden. These words from Heaven have given me comfort, confirmation, encouragement, and strength—especially when facing those unusual times of intense trial and troublesome stress.

I PRAY FOR YOU, DEAR FRIEND

I pray for you, dear friend, that you will find your private garden, a place to meet with the Lord and hear His instructive and revelatory words to your heart. I pray that you will learn to swim in the stream of God's Word, and drink from the waters of God's Spirit as He brings you affectionate prophetic words from heaven.

You ask, "How can I get prophetic words from the Lord?"

Start with God's Word. Get to know the nature and character of God as they are revealed in His Word. Find a translation of the Bible you enjoy. I like the New Living Translation for my devotional reading. Ask the Holy Spirit to enlighten certain passages to you that may be particularly helpful to you now or in the future. Ask that the "logos" words (general words) will become "rhema" words (specific words for you). Then speak those words. They are God's personal Words to you.

Keep a prayer and meditations journal. Write down the prayer thoughts that the Holy Spirit reveals to you and review them often.

God longs to enjoy a deep, intimate relationship with you. If you know Jesus Christ as your Lord, you already know the peace that comes when you are certain your sins have been forgiven, and that a new nature has been implanted within you. You have everything you need to hear prophetic words from heaven. You possess the capacity to experience the wonder of your own private garden. In 1 Corinthians 14:31, St. Paul said, "You may all prophesy . . . ." "All" means you too!

If you would like to learn more about hearing and recognizing God's voice, I encourage you to read my books ***Have You Heard From the Lord Lately?*** and ***Filled***. These books will enrich your understanding of how the Holy Spirit speaks to us today.

May God deeply encourage you on your pathway to the private garden.

"You can step into your own private garden anytime, anywhere. You will be refreshed, educated, and equipped."

ABOUT DAVE WILLIAMS, D.MIN.

Dave Williams is pastor of Mount Hope Church and International Outreach Ministries, with outreach headquarters in Lansing, Michigan. He has pastored there for over 25 years, leading the church from 226 to over 4,000 members today.

The ministry campus comprises 60 acres in Delta Township, Michigan, and includes a multi-million dollar worship center, Bible Training Institute, children's center, youth facilities, Garden Prayer Chapel, Global Prayer Center, Gym and Fitness Center, Care facilities, and a medical complex.

Construction was completed in 2003 of Gilead Healing Center, a multi-million dollar complex that includes medical facilities, nutritional education, and fitness training. Its most important mission is to equip believers to minister to the sick as Jesus and His disciples did. Medical and osteopathic doctors, and doctors of chiropractic and naturopathy all work harmoniously with trained prayer teams to bring about miraculous healing for suffering people from all over the United States.

Under Dave's leadership, 41 daughter and branch churches have been successfully planted in Michigan, the Philippines,

Ghana, Ivory Coast, and Zimbabwe. Including all branch churches, Mount Hope Churches claim over 14,000 members as of December 2005.

Dave is founder and president of Mount Hope Bible Training Institute, a fully-accredited, church-based leadership institute for training ministers, church planters, and lay people to perform the work of the ministry. Dave established and leads the Dave Williams School for Church Planters, located in St. Pete Beach, Florida.

He has authored 53 books including fifteen-time bestseller, ***The New Life . . . The Start of Something Wonderful*** (with over 2 million books sold in eight languages). More recently, he authored ***The World Beyond: The Mysteries of Heaven and How to Get There*** (over 100,000 copies sold). ***Radical Riches***, was a Barnes and Noble top seller for 10 consecutive months. His ***Miracle Results of Fasting*** (Harrison House Publishers) was an Amazon.com five-star top seller for two years in a row.

Dave's articles and reviews have appeared in national magazines such as ***Advance***, ***Pentecostal Evangel***, ***Charisma***, ***Ministries Today***, ***Lansing Magazine***, ***Detroit Free Press***, ***World News***, and others.

According to the Nielsen ratings, Dave's television program, "The Pacesetter's Path," is the number one viewed religious program on both ABC and CBS affiliates in Michigan. He has appeared on national television in the United States and Canada, and has been seen worldwide over "Billy Graham's Decision Network." His television ministry is viewed worldwide over eleven satellite systems and is broadcast 44 times weekly.

Along with his wife, Mary Jo, Dave established The Dave and Mary Jo Williams Charitable Mission (Strategic Global Mission), a non-profit foundation providing scholarships to pioneer pastors and ministry students, as well as grants to inner-city children's ministries.

Dave, as a private pilot, flies for fun. He is married, has two grown children, and lives in Delta Township, Michigan.

CONTACT INFORMATION

Mount Hope Church and International Outreach Ministries
202 S. Creyts Road
Lansing, Michigan 48917

For a complete list of Dave Williams' life-changing books, CDs and videos call:

Phone: 517-321-2780
800-888-7284
TDD: 517-321-8200

or go to our web site:
www.mounthopechurch.org

For prayer requests, call the
Mount Hope Global Prayer Center
24 hour prayer line at:
517-327-PRAY
(517-327-7729)

3 SIGNATURE BOOKS BY DAVE WILLIAMS

:MERGING LEADERS—They are vall breakers and city takers! Don't try to top them. They are unstoppable. Don't ry to understand them. They are often unorthodox in their approach. They are :MERGING LEADERS—a new breed of hurch leadership for the 21st century, and 'ou can be one of them! $12.95

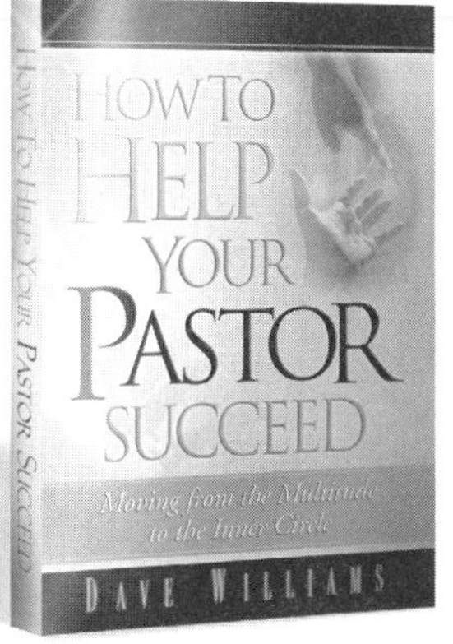

HOW TO HELP YOUR PASTOR SUCCEED—This book leads you to spiritual and practical truths that will help you become your pastor's MVP (Most Valuable Person). It will profoundly and positively affect your life and ministry! $12.95

:OMING INTO THE WEALTHY 'LACE—God wants you to be able to abound to every good work." You need to earn how to release God's power in your fe to get wealth. This book will show you ow to go through the door of just good nough into *The Wealthy Place*! $14.95

TO ORDER, CALL 1-800-888-7284, OR VISIT US ON THE WEB AT: WWW.MOUNTHOPECHURCH.ORG